Japan Style

architecture + interiors + design

introduction by Geeta Mehta
text by Kimie Tada and Geeta Mehta
photographs by Noboru Murata

TUTTLE

Published Tuttle Publishing, an imprint of Periplus
Editions (HK) Ltd, with editorial offices at
364 Innovation Drive, North Clarendon,
Vermont 05759 USA and 61 Tai Seng Avenue,
#02-12, Singapore 534167

LCC Card No: 2005298891
ISBN 978-0-8048-3592-3
ISBN 978-4-8053-0733-5 (for sale in Japan only)

Distributed by:
North America, Latin America & Europe
Tuttle Publishing, 364 Innovation Drive,
North Clarendon, VT 05759-9436, USA
Tel: 1 (802) 773-8930; Fax: 1 (802) 773-6993
info@tuttlepublishing.com
www.tuttlepublishing.com

Asia Pacific
Berkeley Books Pte Ltd, 61 Tai Seng Avenue,
#02-12, Singapore 534167
Tel: (65) 6280 1330; Fax: (65) 6280 6290
inquiries@periplus.com.sg
www.periplus.com.sg

Japan
Tuttle Publishing, Yaekari Building, 3rd Floor,
5-4-12 Osaki, Shinagawa-ku,
Tokyo 141 0032
Tel: (81) 03 5437-0171; Fax: (81) 03 5437-0755
tuttle-sales@gol.com

Front cover: The focus of traditional Japanese design
is on space, and on how each object placed in space
changes it dynamically. Architectural details are often
bold, but designed so as to not detract from this space.

Back cover: The room seen through this single pan-
eled screen (*tsuitate*) is a mere five square meters in
area, but appears expansive due to the use of simple
low furniture and uncluttered lines.

Half-title page: Japanese design strives to achieve a
dynamic balance in ikebana as well as other arts. The
concept of symmetry, so important to Western design,
is considered static, and consciously avoided in Japan.
Title page: Lit from underneath, the glass floor of the
tokonoma alcove adds a dramatic modern note to the
otherwise traditional muted colors and natural materials
of this room.

This page: Furniture—such as this display alcove,
shelves and cupboards—are built into the room
to achieve unobstructed space. The bold dark lines
of the wood frames and tatami mat borders work
with vertical and horizontal planes to create an
intensely calm effect.

Printed in Hong Kong.

10 09 08   6 5 4 3

CONTENTS

What is Japanese about a Japanese House?

A surprising intellectual leap in housing design took place in Japan during the 14th century. This was an idea so powerful that it resonated for the next 600 years, and still retains enough influence in Japan as shown in the houses in this book. This intellectual leap sought to "eliminate the inessential," and seek the beauty in unembellished humble things. It sought spaciousness in deliberately small spaces, and a feeling of eternity in fragile and temporary materials. A house's interior was not to be just protected from nature, but to be integrated with nature in harmony. Influential Zen Buddhist priests in the Muromachi and Momoyama Periods articulated this ideal so well that thought leaders in many fields followed it, and the entire Japanese society aspired to it. What resulted were homes that speak to the soul and seem to hold time still. They provide a quiet simple base from which to deal with the world.

Around the time that European and English homes were becoming crammed with exotic bric-a-brac collected from the newly established colonies, Japanese Zen priests were sweeping away even the furniture from their homes. Out also went any overt decorations. What was left was a simple flexible space that could be used according to the needs of the hour. At night the bedrolls were taken from deep *oshire* cupboards, and during the day they were replaced, making space for meals, work, play and entertaining. This "lightness" was in part a response to Japan's frequent earthquakes, and in part to the Buddhist teachings about the transient nature of all things. It is interesting to note that this ephemerality is not reflected in the architectural tradition in India, China or Korea, the three countries from where Buddhism arrived in Japan.

Wood is the preferred building material in Japan. The country's Shinto roots have inculcated a deep understanding of and respect for nature. Japanese carpenters have perfected techniques of drawing out the intrinsic beauty of wood. Craftsmen often feel, smell and sometimes even taste wood before purchasing it. Although stone is available in abundance in mountainous Japan, it was traditionally used for the foundations of temples, castles and, to a limited extent, for homes and warehouses. Even brick buildings, when first built in Ginza around 1870, stayed untenanted for a long time, because people preferred to live in well ventilated wooden buildings.

Traditional Japanese builders designed houses from the inside out, the way modern architects professed to do until about two decades ago. A house's exterior evolved from its plan, rather then being forced into pre-conceived symmetrical forms. Bruno Taut, a German architect trained at Bauhaus, and who came to Japan in 1933, claimed that "Japanese architecture has always been modern." The Bauhaus mantras of "form follows function" and "less is more," as well as the "modern" ideas of modular grids, prefabrication and standardization had long been part of Japanese building traditions.

Minimalism and simplicity are the hallmarks of Zen-inspired traditional Japanese interiors. This effect is achieved by a rhythm of vertical and horizontal surfaces paired with natural colors. Exterior wall panels and *shoji* screens have been removed in this room to let the summer breeze and garden view in, making it "as open as a tent."

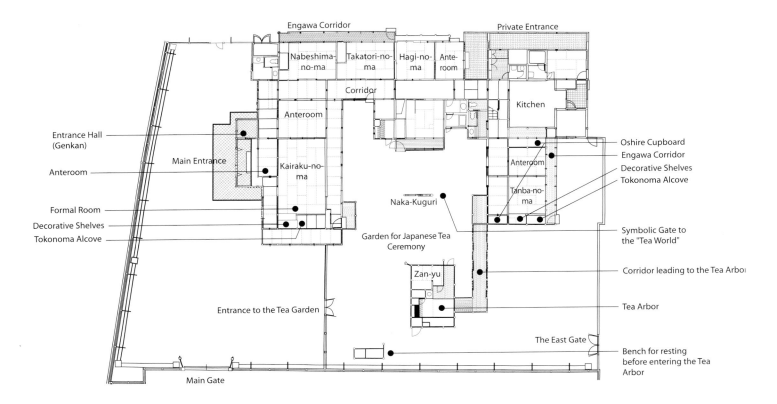

Floor-plan of Zan Yu So—the organic organization of a Japanese house

Around the time when Leonardo da Vinci was developing a system of dimensions that scaled the human body for use in architecture, Japanese craftsmen standardized the dimensions of a tatami mat to 90 x 180 centimeters, which was considered adequate for a Japanese person to sleep on. Every dimension in a Japanese house relates to the module of a tatami mat. For example, the height of *fusuma* doors is usually 180 centimeters. The width of a structural post is usually one-tenth or one-fifth of 90 centimeters, and the post's bevel is one-seventh or one-tenth of its width. Thus, as in da Vinci's model, the proportions and scale of a traditional Japanese house can be considered to flow from the dimensions of the human body.

The houses shown in this book are a wonderful reminder that there are other alternatives to "big is beautiful," and that eternity is not about permanent materials. Living in the "condensed" world—Japan's population is half the size of the US, but it occupies a land area about 30 times smaller—the Japanese have developed a unique understanding of space. An ikebana arrangement charges the area in and around itself, and that space becomes an integral part of the design. The arrangement would not be nearly as effective without this empty space. One of the most famous buildings in Japan is the Taien tea hut built by

Sen no Rikyu, the famous 16th century tea master. This masterpiece of Japanese architecture measures a mere one-and-three-quarters of a tatami mat, or approximately three square meters. This tiny house gives an example of how small houses do not have to take the form of the proverbial "rabbit hutches," but can be beautiful and open like the Kamikozawa home (pages 178–183) and the house owned by Toru Baba and Keiko Asou (pages 98–107). After all, how much space does a man need?

Traditional Japanese houses have a special relationship with nature. In extreme cases, the best part of a lot was given over to the garden, and the house designed on the land left over. Entire *shoji* walls can be pushed aside, creating an intimate unity with the garden. The *engawa* corridor modulates the relationship between the house's interior and exterior. In summer, it belongs to the outdoors, while in winter and at night it is closed off to form part of the interior space as shown in the Zan Yu So villa (page 20–37).

The wood-floored *engawa* corridor mediates the relationship between the interior and exterior of a room. The storm shutters on the outer edge of the *engawa* are removed during the day so that the veranda becomes part of the garden, while at night, or during stormy weather, the shutters are closed to extend the interior space. These wooden storm shutters are a feature many newer houses in Japan do not have.

As pointed out by architect Antonin Raymond, who came to Japan to work with Frank Lloyd Wright, "The Japanese house is surprisingly free. At night and in the winter, one can shut out the world and the interior becomes a box divided up into rooms. Then in the summer, one opens up all the storm doors, the sliding screens and sliding doors and the house becomes as free as a tent through which air gently passes." Made of wood, mud and straw, the traditional house is also environmentally friendly and recyclable. Even old tatami mats can be shredded and composted.

Another facet of the Japanese house, and indeed of Japanese life, is the dichotomy between the private and the public. In narrow but deep townhouses like Kondaya Genbei (pages 38–51), public dealings were confined to the house's street side, while the rooms beyond were reserved for domestic life. The Japanese word for depth is *oku*, so a wife is referred to as *oku-san*, "the lady who inhabits a house's depths." How far into the home a guest penetrates depends on his relationship with the family. A house has a "public face," which may or may not convey anything about the

hidden interior. Powerful feudal lords often chose to live in the simple, understated Sukiya-style spaces, while visitors would only see the ornate staterooms. However, the private areas allowed for little privacy, since mere paper screens or thin walls separated the rooms from each other. This fact has probably contributed to the deeply ingrained sociable manners in Japanese people, especially women.

Types of Japanese Houses and Interiors

This book focuses on several types of houses and interiors. Yamamoto's *minka* (pages 108–119) is a good example of Japan's rustic farmhouses, which were functional and built of sturdy local materials. Such a house can be generally divided into two distinct zones. The entrance area (about one-third of the space) is called a *doma*, and has a packed earthen floor. A family would cook, produce crafts and in very cold climates, also tether farm animals here at night. The farmhouse's second zone usually stands on a wooden plinth and includes the living area and bedrooms. The large hearth at the heart of the main room was the hub of family activity in such homes, the beauty of which is derived from rustic materials such as unhewn timbers and from the integrity of ancient building techniques. The heavy roof with deep eaves on these farmhouses, which often constitutes two-thirds of the elevation, makes them appear comfortably rooted in their surroundings. Frank Lloyd Wright considered

Above: Simple interior surfaces and spaces add drama to the few objects d'art displayed in a room.

Left: The unassuming beauty of a *minka* farmhouse comes from natural materials such as unhewn logs, mud, bamboo and straw. Traditional building methods, perfected over hundreds of years, are employed to create a building that is ecologically sustainable and completely recyclable.

the *minka* an appropriate symbol of domestic stability, and they became one of the several Japanese ideas that influenced his residential designs.

Most of the houses in this book were built in an urban context. The larger homes, such as the Tsai house (pages 120–131), are located in the countryside, but have a strong emphasis on formality, and are built in the Shoin or Sukiya–Shoin style like their urban counterparts. Elements of these houses have evolved from the rigid Shinden style that was borrowed and adapted from China during the eighth century. This style consisted of a central chamber reserved for the master of the house, with corridors, smaller rooms for the family and pavilions that flanked this room, all arranged around a small pond or a garden. During the Muromachi Period (1336–1572), the Shinden style evolved into the Japanese Shoin style, used for the reception rooms of the aristocracy and the samurai classes, but which was banned in the homes of common people during the Edo Period (1600–1867). This style includes four distinct elements that have been formalized over time: the decorative alcove (*tokonoma*) for hanging scrolls and other objects; staggered shelves (*chigaidana*) located next the *tokonoma*; decorative doors known as *chodaigamae*; and a built-in desk

This large country house and its garden are seen here through the perimeter fence. Built with natural materials and colors, the house nestles comfortably in the garden that attempts to mimic the great outdoors as closely as possible. The ethos is of co-existence with nature, not control over it.

(*tsuke shoin*) that usually juts out into the *engawa*, flanked by *shoiji* paper screens. All these features started out as pieces of loose furniture, but were built in over time, in keeping with the Japanese preference for clean, uninterrupted spaces. Tatami mats usually cover the entire floor in these formal rooms.

As the tea ceremony increased in popularity during the Muromachi, Momoyama and Edo Periods, the ideal of the humble tea hut began to exercise a strong influence on Japanese housing design. Ostentatious Shoin-style interiors gave way to the more relaxed Sukiya–Shoin style in all but the most formal residences. Sukiya style turned all the rules of the rigid Shoin style inside out, and provided abundant opportunities for personal expression. It sought beauty in the passage of time, as seen in the decay of delicate natural materials in an interior and the growth of moss on tree trunks and stones in a garden. While the rest of the world searched for the most durable and ornate building materials, Japan's elite were scouring their forests for fragile-looking pieces of wood that would underscore the imperfection of things. The moth-eaten wood selected by Baizan Nakamura for his cabinet doors (pages 172–173) is an example of this trend. The ideal of *wabi-sabi*, translated loosely by Frank Lloyd Wright as "rusticity and simplicity that borders on

loneliness," was considered the epitome of sophistication. For interiors, Sukiya style also favored asymmetrical arrangements, while avoiding repetition and symmetry. Posts on walls were arranged so as not to divide a wall space into equal parts. A variety of woods were used for different parts of the same structure to add interest. However, such diversity results in a satisfying whole because of the discipline of horizontal and vertical lines and muted soft colors. The goal is to please rather than impress the visitor. The owners of these houses participated in the selection of materials and playful design details such as doorknobs and nail covers.

Sukiya–Shoin rooms are often complemented by tea huts in their gardens. It was not unusual for architects and designers to make full-scale paper models (*okoshiezu*) of a tea hut to perfect its designs before the actual construction process began.

Above: These small tea ceremony utensils underscore the attention to detail in Japanese design. At left are two whisks referred to as *chasen*; one has been turned over on a stand especially designed for that purpose. The flat scoop (*chashaku*), is an object of art in its own right. During the Momoyama and Edo Periods, men of power often vied with each other in crafting this simple object.

Right: Japanese and modern Western elements of this interior complement each other, since both aspire to the beauty of simplicity. The *shoji* wall on the left is completely removable.

Five of the houses in this book were not built with traditional materials and techniques, but have nonetheless been included because they express the dynamics of Japanese space and sensibilities. Although traditional houses are decreasing in number, traditional spatial concepts inform the work of many contemporary architects in Japan. While most Japanese now live in apartments or modern homes that are usually small but comfortable, they maintain deep pride and love for their traditional architecture. With growing awareness of the many wonderful buildings already lost to the recent development frenzy, there is now renewed interest in saving traditional structures. Several homes in this book were moved to new locations for preservation—a very encouraging sign. I hope that this book will strengthen this trend.

The houses featured in this book are important not just for the Japanese but also for all of us. They invite us to rethink the wisdom of our unsustainable lifestyles. Contrary to Le Corbusier's adage of modern architecture, a traditional Japanese house is not simply a "machine to live in," but a home for the soul.

The focus on Japanese design is not on surfaces, but on the quality of the resulting space. This modern Japanese house achieves the feeling of traditional Japanese space with modern materials and furniture.

A Tea Master's Dream Lives On

Sado or the "Way of Tea" seeks to extend the meditative simplicity of the tea ceremony or *chanoyu* into all aspects of life. The ideal of a mind in complete harmony with nature and free from the turmoil of worldly affairs has blossomed in Japan since Zen Buddhism arrived here from India and China in the 13th century. From the Meiji Era (1868–1912) to the early Showa Period (1926–1989), many influential people in political and financial circles became particularly strong proponents of *chanoyu*, as they searched for balance in their secular and spiritual lives. This helped the ideals of *chanoyu* strongly influence many arts in Japan including architecture, painting, pottery, poetry, calligraphy and flower arrangement. In architecture, *chanoyu* has generated a special style called the Sukiya style, known for its minimalism, simplicity, rusticity, understatement and a restrained playfulness. The Takamatsu house was built in 1917 in the Sukiya style by Teiichi Takamatsu, a renowned votary of *chanoyu* in Nagoya district, located between Tokyo and Kyoto. The second-generation head of a wealthy family that owns substantial real estate, he brought his profound love of *chanoyu* to the building of his house. After his son inherited the family business and his father's beloved residence, this house became the setting for many dramas in the financial scene of Japan for the next several decades.

This historic legacy nearly came to an end when the house was slated for destruction in 1985. Fortunately, Teruyuki Yamazaki, a businessman with a deep understanding of Japanese architecture, helped save this invaluable Sukiya-style house by purchasing it as a guest house for his company. The new owner was moved by the fact that the Takamatsu house was nearly as old as his machine tool exporting company, Yamazaki Mazak Corp., which was founded in 1919, and had witnessed the same historic developments.

Yamazaki relocated the Takamatsu house—which was relatively easy to do, since traditional Japanese homes are made of skillful wood joinery—to a scenic part of the Aichi Prefecture on a generous 6,700 square meter plot with a good view of the Kiso River. It has now been renamed Zan Yu So, which literally means, "a villa to enjoy oneself for a while." The rebuilding of the Takamatsu house was completed in 1990 after five years of reconstruction, involving just a few changes necessitated due to its move. Besides the grand reception room of this house, which has 20 tatami mats, there are several ten-mat rooms, each one with a different theme and an elaborate interior. All the rooms offer picture-perfect views of the lovely garden, which also has a special tearoom connected to the house via a passage. In keeping with the true Sukiya aesthetics of understatement, this large house has an air of modest elegance rather than showy pride. Its natural simplicity and a sense of stillness are still spiritually uplifting, in keeping with what the original owner might have intended.

Above: A cupboard for storing shoes is an essential feature of a *genkan*, the entrance for welcoming guests. The sliding doors here are covered with paper with the special pattern usually reserved for larger sliding doors called *fusuma*.

Left: Slippers await guests in the *genkan* of Zan Yu So. Changing from shoes worn outside the house to slippers is symbolic of getting into a more relaxed state of mind. The quiet lines and understated material of this new entrance have been carefully designed to harmonize with the old reconstructed house.

Overleaf: The relationship between the interior and the garden is very important in Japanese architecture. The gardens are designed to be viewed from the low vantage point of a person seated in the room on a tatami mat. Here the *shoji* screens have been slid aside to open the drawing room to the beautiful garden. The roofed gate (*naka-kuguri*) and the tearoom are visible on the right of a grand Japanese oak tree. The panel on top of the *shoji* screens (*ranma*) is known as *muso mado*—one perforated panel slides behind the other, opening or closing the apertures to suit the different ventilation needs of changing seasons.

Above: An arrangement of open shelves (*tsuri-dana*) and low storage compartments (*ji-bukuro*) in the recess adjoining the *tokonoma* is part of the traditional Shoin-style décor.

Left: The small stand and the writing case (*suzuri-bako*) is beautifully decorated by exquisite artwork known as *maki-e*. In this technique, a design with lacquer and fine specks of gold and silver is painted in several layers on a prepared wooden surface.

Opposite: The grand reception room, Kairaku-no-ma, is decorated in Shoin style. This interior design style was originally named after the built-in writing desks (*tsuke shoin*) in the rooms of Zen priests. Since then, a built-in desk and the accompanying *shoji* window have become ceremonial elements of formal décor, as seen in this room. The deep *tokonoma*, another element of the formal Shoin style, holds a *cha-ire*—a pot for preserving green tea— that had been a gift from Tsunayoshi, the fourth Tokugawa Shogun, to one of his vassals. The hanging *kakejiku* was painted by Tanyu Kano (1602–1674), a renowned painter of the Kano school, which supplied the Shoguns with their official painters for as long as 300 years.

Above: The *tokonoma* alcove in a tearoom named
Zanyu is decorated by a hanging scroll (*kakejiku*)
with five Chinese characters which represent prosperity. On the left of the *tokonoma* is the "sleeve
wall" that separates the tearoom from the host's
entrance. The post at the end of this half wall is
called *nakabashira*, or the central pillar, and this
as well as the corner post in the *tokonoma* alcove
(*toko-bashira*) is selected with great care as they set
the aesthetic mood of the tearoom.

Right: The square entrance to the tearoom, called
nijiri guchi, is made very small, just 60 centimeters
high in this case. The traditional reason for making
the guests enter the tearoom on their hands and
knees was to make them leave their swords and
egos behind, coming in with a humble and pure
mind. The soft outline of *shitaji mado*, the bamboo
and reed lattice is seen through the *shoji* screen.
Japanese paper (*washi*) is pasted to the lower portion of the walls (*koshibari*) to protect the guest's
kimonos from the mud plaster on the walls.

Above: Utensils used in the tea ceremony are made of bamboo. At left are the whisks (*chasen*), used to briskly stir the green tea (*matcha*) in the teacup with the hot water. The flat scoop, called *chashaku*, is used to measure the powdered green tea into the tea bowl. The flat toothpicks (*kuromoji*) are used by guests to eat Japanese sweets during a tea ceremony. The guests often bring their own *kuromoji*, along with Japanese paper napkins, in a special bag tucked inside the collar of their kimonos when they arrive for the tea ceremony.

Left: A humble hook is provided on a post in the small kitchen (*mizuya*) for hanging the tea cloth.

Opposite: This *mizuya* with a cupboard for tea utensils and a sink in which to wash them adjoins a formal area. Every little detail is thought through and made as beautiful as possible. The floor-level sink covered with a bamboo mat is one example of this attention to detail.

Above: The veranda (*engawa*) modulates the area between the inner and outer zones, allowing sunlight into the house and protecting it from rain. In summer it forms part of the garden; in the winter the *engawa* can be closed off to form an extension of the interior space.

Left: A path of stepping-stones, also called "dewy path" or *roji*, leading to the tea hut is seen here through the glass window. A simple gate (*nakakuguri*) in the middle of the garden separates the inner and outer tea garden. Passing through the middle gate is symbolic of entering the tea world. Moss is a prized element of a tea garden and is carefully cultivated.

Above: The large panel in this *tokonoma* (*toko-ita*) measures 360 centimeters across and is made from a single piece of very rare pinewood.

Left: The *toko-bashira*, or the main post between the *tokonoma* and *chigaidana*, is made of northern Japanese magnolia wood, and has been selected for its artistic effect. The ceiling made from a variety of woods, paper and reeds adds an air of rustic elegance to this anteroom.

Right top, middle and below: The door pulls (*hikite*) —depicting a pigeon (top), a peacock (middle) and a boat oar (bottom)—are selected to suit the theme of the room. The peacock *hikite* is fashioned from lacquer and real gold.

Above: The alcove in a room named Takatori-no-ma has a fine post (*toko-bashira*) made of *kitayama-sugi*, a very high-quality wood. The wall on the side of the alcove has a window with a graceful bamboo lattice in an unusual diagonal pattern.

Left: A small wooden case (*suzuri-bako*) holds an ink stone, an ink stick, a brush and a tiny water bottle used for mixing ink.

Opposite: Rooms designed in a manner less formal than the Shoin style are referred to as *hira-shoin* rooms. The lower part of this *hira-shoin* has a sliding slat window (*muso mado*). The checkered openings on the front and back slats can be lined up to allow for air circulation.

Summer Style in a Kyoto Machiya

Located in the heart of Kyoto, the Imperial capital of Japan for over 400 years, Kondaya Genbei is an excellent example of an elegant Kyoto-style *machiya*, or merchant's townhouse. Muromachi, the district where this townhouse is located, was once a powerful trade center known for its aristocratic tastes and many elegant buildings. Kondaya Genbei was established in the 1730s and has since served as a residence and a shop where traditional kimonos and obi sashes are crafted and sold. The prosperous business is presently run by the tenth generation owner, Genbei Yamaguchi, who is also a kimono designer himself. In 2002, he helped revive a species of silk cocoons called *koishimaru*. These cocoons was used in ancient Japan for making a delicate variety of silk capable of taking on vivid dyes, but had been replaced with larger cocoons because they were too small for the efficient production of silk. Due to Genbei Yamaguchi's efforts, silk of this sort is in production again after a hiatus of many decades.

This two-storey timber building sits on a deep rectangular lot along the street, with a 30-meter façade several times larger than the neighboring lots. Narrow frontages are typical of *machiya* since the properties were taxed based upon the width of their street fronts. The outside of the house is made up of wooden lattice painted with Bengala, a reddish colcothar so named because it was first imported from Bengal in India. The entrance leads into a *doma*, a room with an earthen floor, used for casual meetings or the receiving of supplies. One does not need to take shoes off here. Rooms beyond this one are raised on a wooden plinth and get more sophisticated and private along the *tori-niwa* corridor leading into the house. The inner part of the house also contains a small garden (*tsubo-niwa*), a tearoom (*cha-shitsu*) and two storerooms (*kura*). The *tsubo-niwa* helps ventilate the interior, while bringing nature in. The storerooms, set apart from the main house, are protected by heavy, fire-resistant plaster walls. Merchandise and family treasures are stored in them to this very day.

In Japanese culture, food, clothing as well as décor reflect the changing seasons. Kyotoites have traditionally delighted in changing the décor of their homes to create an ambience of coolness during the warm summers. The Yamaguchis observe this vanishing custom by removing the *shoji* and *fusuma* paper screens of their home, replacing them with woven wooden frames (*sudo*) draped with beautifully woven bamboo blinds (*sudare*). The open weave of the *sudo* blurs the division between interior and exterior, allowing residents to look out, while letting light and breeze in. Through these screens, the rays of the summer sun appear soft as twilight, and the moiré-like pattern cast by overlapping *sudo* reminds one of a cool rippling pond. A closely woven rattan rug made from Indonesian cane (*tou-ajir*) is laid over tatami mats, and the dark sheen it acquires over time is associated with a perception of coolness. Summer in Kyoto also heralds the coming of the famous Gion Festival—which dates back to 869 AD—and the Yamaguchis continue the tradition of old families who displayed special heirlooms such as *byobu*, armor and kimonos that are in the theme of this festival in their home during this time of the year.

Above: Before approaching the tearoom, guests make a ritual stop at the water basin in a tea garden to wash their hands and purify their spirit.

Left: Tearooms are made intentionally small and plain, so as not to distract from the important goal of achieving harmony within oneself. This tearoom is of four-and-a-half tatami mats, a popular size that refers to the *hojo*—the quarters of Zen abbots—so named after the humble hut of a sage in India that Buddha is said to have visited. The tea garden can be seen through the *sudo* screens on the window.

Above: The walk along the dewy path (*roji*) is occasionally interrupted at a turn by an odd stone (*tobi ishi*), which forces one to look down to ensure balance. Then the refreshed eyes look up to see a special accent such a stone lantern (*toro*). The moss and bushes are tended every day to keep the garden looking fresh. This, like the freshly watered *roji*, is a sign of welcome for the guests.

Right: During the Gion Festival, which runs the entire month of July, old families follow the tradition of inviting guests to their formal room where folding screens (*byobu*), kimono and armors are displayed. This pair of six-paneled early 18th century screens with hawks was painted by Tsunenobu Kano of the famous Kano school. The flower arrangement in the bamboo container gently demarcates the area accessible to guests.

Previous pages: In summer, an ice column placed on a wooden veranda (*engawa*) provides natural air-conditioning as well as a treat for the eyes. The Yamaguchis replace teacups and pots made of ceramics with glass ones during the summer, placing them on coasters made of reeds. The rattan rug laid on the tatami mats has a wattle pattern, which enhances the suggestion of coolness. The *shoji* screens have also been replaced by openwork *sudare* blinds. The basket has a flat paper fan (*uchiwa*) with a design of kabuki make-up.

Above: A sculpture depicting eggplant fruit and flowers sits on the writing desk (*tsuke shoin*), while light streams in from *sudo* screens.

Right: The ears of rice and *sakaki* leaves in the alcove (*tokonoma*) form a display reflecting the ritual decoration of floats paraded in the Gion Festival. *Koishimaru* are placed on a small offering stand (*sanbo*) made of wood.

Above left: This corridor leads to the formal room (*zashiki*). On the right is the corridor that connects to the tearoom.

Above right: Guests can choose to approach the tearoom via the covered walkway or they can put on wooden clogs (*geta*), and walk along the meandering stepping-stones in the tea garden.

Left: This tatami room opens onto the earthen-floored corridor leading to the entrance porch. Seasonal flowers are laid out in preparation for ikebana. The *fusuma* paper has a design of orchid flowers, block-printed by hand using iridescent mica paint.

Above: A bellflower is placed at the far end of
the upstairs hallway in an asymmetric arrangement
invoking natural growth, a feature typical of ikebana.

Right: The quiet empty space around the flower
arrangement and the hanging scroll in the *tokonoma*
is charged with the presence of these elements,
and therefore is an essential part of the display.

Exuberant Spontaneity in an Interior in Osaka

While *wabi-sabi* simplicity and understatement are the hallmarks of Kyoto style, interiors in Osaka often bustle with exuberance and spontaneity. This is well illustrated by Teizo Sato who imparts his innovative and playful spirit to the interiors of his house. The house is situated in an upscale residential area near the Fujiidera Stadium in Osaka. His grandfather built the house over 70 years ago, using Japanese hemlock, which was a popular material for luxurious homes at that time. Over time, the surfaces of hemlock timber as well as the garden have acquired a wonderful patina and a welcoming air.

The Japanese describe a person who is free from the trammels of ordinary life and able to deeply admire the beauty of nature, as well as things, as being *furyu*. Teizo Sato, a bachelor who is adept at the tea ceremony and Japanese flower arrangement, likes to think of himself as such a person. Having lived among beautiful antiques in this special house since he was six, he has cultivated a discerning eye and an understanding of Eastern as well as Western aesthetics, and often mixes the two with great panache.

Like many pottery enthusiasts, one of Sato's favorite collections is that of soba cups. Soba, or buckwheat noodles, are served on a wickerwork platter and eaten with a dipping sauce served in soba cups. Sato scours curio shops and antique markets after work and on every weekend, sometimes traveling as far as Tokyo to look for cups with special designs. In order to truly enjoy the cups and other tableware he has collected, he has taken to cooking and delights in setting the table with his favorite dishes. His enthusiasm for collecting and using antiques also extends to earthenware, glassware, fabrics, furniture and Buddhist paintings.

Sato enjoys creating innovative interior arrangements to entertain and surprise his guests, while telling them stories related to his displays. Although it is common to see only minimum or restrained decoration in Sukiya-style interiors, Sato's displays are just the opposite, overflowing with new ideas and nuances. He also likes to use *byobu*, or folding screens, as decorative elements, as a backdrop for his displays, and as versatile dividers for his interiors. Japan has several festivals throughout the year such as the New Year, the Girls' (Dolls') Festival, the Boys' Festival, the Star Festival and the Chrysanthemum Festival. On these and other special occasions, Sato creates interior arrangements with appropriate festive themes. He hangs scrolls with paintings or calligraphic works in the *tokonoma* alcove to suit each festival. The highlight of such decorations is his display of dolls for the Girls' Festival on March 3 each year, when Sato's home comes alive with dolls and flowers, and is opened to the public for three days. The tradition of this annual exhibition in the Sato house is already 20 years old and becoming widely known, attracting as many as 3,000 spectators each year. Hopefully this old home will continue to host this show for many years to come.

Left: In this unconventionally bold vestibule, a closely woven carpet (*nabeshima-jutan*) is set in front of gorgeous *fusuma* doors. The pot on the antique chest is from the Korean Joseon Dynasty (1392–1910), referred to as Richo in Japan. Its circular form is echoed in the Oribe-ware plate on the shelf below.

Previous pages: The Sato house nestles in an abundance of natural greenery, dotted with the family's collection of stone lanterns (*toro*).

Above: Staggered shelves (*chigaidana*) for displaying art objects are usually built beside the *tokonoma* in formal interiors. Here, a red lacquer bamboo-woven container (*rantai-shikki*) sits in the foreground. On the left stands an Edo Period (1600–1867) *oi* backpack in which itinerant Buddhist monks carried their sutra scrolls.

Left: The alcove, which is rendered in fine black sand, holds a hanging scroll (*kakejiku*) from Taizan in China. The three kanji characters represent affluence and happiness. A leather hat from the Edo Period, formerly worn by common foot soldiers in place of helmets serves as a vase for a clematis bud.

Above: The folding screen (*byobu*) patterned with fans is used as a striking backdrop for a splendid, red lacquered low table. Sake bottles, bowls and plates have been set for guests.

Right: The collection of papier-mâché dolls rests on open shelves softly lit by the surrounding *shoji* screen. Such dolls have been made in Fukushima Prefecture since the Edo Period (1600–1867).

Above: This room attempts to combine Japanese sensibilities with Western-style decor. Antique Koimari ware is intermingled with modern pieces.

Left: An octagonal tray with legs from the Korean Joseon Dynasty (1392–1910), an antique Imari pot, and a 19th century Western-style lamp all seem at home in this corner of the veranda.

Opposite: The L-shaped veranda (*engawa*) provides the characteristic intermediate space between the interior and the garden.

Top: The papier-mâché doll in the top picture represents Ushiwakamaru, a popular 12th century general, who is still regarded as a hero in Japan.

Above: These ornamental battledores, made in the early 20th century, are of the kind traditionally used for playing badminton during the New Year's holiday.

Left: The picture shows the same room seen in the previous pages, transformed in a flourish by the innovative owner to display a seasonal arrangement of peonies and maple leaves. The open-shelf *ranma* near the ceiling above the two antique *tansu* chests hosts his large collection of blue and white soba cups of various designs.

Previous pages: Irises, maple leaves, temple candle stands and a kimono are displayed against a golden folding screen (*byobu*). The pattern on the kimono is made especially for early summer, and features carp swimming up the waterfalls. Legend has it that the carp can become dragons if they can succeed in reaching the top.

Above: Shrubbery and rocks in a Japanese garden are watered—the dewy garden is a subtle sign of welcome for visitors. The intention is to please rather than impress the visitor.

Right: The *shoji* screens of this room are opened, uniting the garden outside with the interior. The half-moon bridge forms the centerpiece of the arrangement of rocks and plants in the garden. The two Japanese cypress (*hinoki*) were planted by Sato when he was a child. A connoisseur of arts even at that young age, he had planned to someday use them as the *toko-bashira* post—which is made of wood selected for its beauty or special associations—in the *tokonoma* alcove.

House of Ikebana

With lively eyes, good posture and thick gray hair belying her age, Chizu Kusume, who will soon reach her 90th year, is the owner of a home that is imbued with the spirit of ikebana, the Japanese art of arranging flowers. Her house is located in Zushi, an old resort town by the Pacific Ocean in Kanagawa Prefecture. What was a once a sedate vacation destination for many celebrated painters and authors, has now become a busy suburb for commuters working in Tokyo. However, a few traditional buildings, like Kusume's house, have survived the change, and are a good reminder of bygone days.

Kusume's house was built in the early Showa Period (1926–1989) as a simple rental house for holidaymakers, but has acquired an air of dignity and poise over time, quite distinct from its more recent neighbors. Architecturally, it is a rather simple house with no remarkable columns, massive beams, or extraordinary workmanship. However, over the past 60 years, it has become a beautiful antique, something like a simple earthenware piece from ages past. Kusume moved into this small, two-storey 150-square-meter house in 1941. It has a garden over three times the size of the house, which is fairly large by Japanese standards. On opening the wooden sliding door at the entrance, the first thing that catches the eye is the flower arrangement in front of a single panel screen (*tsuitate*), giving a feeling of formality and dignity. The next room is the drawing room (*zashiki*) and the room at the back (*cha-no-ma*) is for Kusume's private use. These two rooms have the deep eaves of the roof and the *engawa* corridor to protect them from strong sunlight, and to provide a transitional space between the indoor and the garden. This transitional space is a special feature of Japanese architecture.

To her credit, Chizu Kusume, who proclaims herself "a devoted admirer of flowers," has taken loving care of the house, infusing it with her aesthetic sense over the years. Ikebana embodies the essence of Japanese aesthetics and a deep respect for nature. Compared to the symmetrical and exuberant arrangements of the West, ikebana strives to use just a few flowers in an asymmetrical balance that is fragile yet so dynamic that moving even one stem would destroy the tight composition. There are many ikebana schools in Japan, each with a distinct philosophy. Kusume has established her own school, Murasaki-Kai (literally translated as the "Purple Group"). Her school's foremost principle is to arrange flowers as they grow in nature, without formalizing or manipulating them.

As she goes about her business of inspiring her students and arranging seasonal flowers every day, Kusume carefully picks out a suitable container for each arrangement from her vast collection of vases, and uses her great sense of design, which she has cultivated over time, to ensure that each arrangement comes alive. A successful ikebana arrangement charges the space in and around itself, so placing the arrangements in each room has to be done with great care so as to provide adequate "breathing room" around them. Like a freshly watered garden, Chizu Kusume's flower arrangements refresh the spirits of the beholder.

Above: The classic chest (*tansu*) with elaborate cast-iron metal work is typical of those used traditionally to store precious belongings that may need to be carried out in a hurry in a fire. The white porcelain jar with chrysanthemums is from the Korean Joseon Dynasty (1392–1910). The photograph is by Denjiro Hasegawa, and depicts the famous sculpture of the Indian god Asura from Kofukuji Temple in Nara.

Left: The room is flooded with sunlight, enhancing the warm tones of tatami. It opens onto the L-shaped veranda (*engawa*), looking beyond it to a pine grove that is typical of this seaside area.

Two tatami rooms are joined when the partitions between are removed. In the *tokonoma* alcove, a chrysanthemum and an ampelopsis are arranged in a decanter made for offering liquor to the gods of the Silla Kingdom (57 BC–935 AD) on the Korean Peninsula. The *yukimi shoji* frames the view outside, screening the top and revealing a beautiful part of the garden through its lower half. The table, known as a *horigotatsu*, has an interesting design. During the winter months, a quilt is placed under a removable table top, above an open wooden frame over which people hang their legs. Family and friends keep warm by putting their legs under the table and the quilt as they dine and relax.

Above: The indoor brazier (*hibachi*) holds an eclectic collection of Kusume's daily utensils—a bird-shaped cigar cutter, a silver pitcher, a cloisonné letter rack and a Baccarat Crystal paperweight from France.

Right: Poised like a still-life picture, persimmons and chayote have been arranged on the low cedar table. The texture of this table is the work of a skilled carpenter who has deepened and emphasized the natural wood grain.

Left: The dressing table with the oval mirror from the Taisho Period (1912–1926) is a good representative of the age when Japan eagerly emulated Western technology and arts. The copper vase bears a toad lily and a bit of pampas grass from the garden.

A Kaga-style Teahouse to Sooth the Soul

Kanazawa, one of the wealthiest castle towns in the Edo Period (1600–1867), was also famous for its elegant culture. Arts such as the tea ceremony flourished under its powerful Maeda lords, and were known for their bold flourishes in comparison with the understated arts in Kyoto. The first stop on the highway that connected Kyoto to Kanazawa Castle was Nonoichi Town in the Kaga area. The Mimou home is situated along the old highway in this town. This stately mansion, along with its various tea-rooms and storehouses, was built by the influential Mimou family in the 1870s, soon after the time of the Meiji Revolution in 1968.

The main Mimou house is built in the Sukiya style, the style of tea ceremony. A tea garden is an integral part of the Sukiya experience, and acts as an interface between the tea hut and the mundane world. The garden has a series of gates or thresholds to punctuate the guests' walk on a *roji* stone path from the outside world to the tea hut. At each such marker, the guest may sit down and relax, releasing worldly cares to enter a "tea state of mind." The plants in the tea garden are designed to be a microcosm of nature in the deep forests, where big evergreen trees grow alongside low shrubs, and the ground is carpeted with thick moss. The views that a guest sees while walking along a mean-dering path on the *roji* are carefully considered, so as to compress the sensory experience of a longer walk in the short distance from entry to the tearoom. The *roji* path finally leads to a large stepping-stone placed in front of the tearoom, usually surrounded by a broad earthen floor under deep eaves.

The eight-mat tearoom in the Mimou house shows a connoisseur's refined taste, and exquisite care taken to heighten the intrinsic beauty of nature. *Shoji* windows and doors are placed and fitted with painstaking consideration for garden views and the lighting conditions during certain hours of the day. Filtered light through thick rice paper gives soft luster to a painting of deer on silvery *fusuma* doors. Handmade white paper, pasted to the lower part of brown-coated walls, reflects the light, adding a bit of brightness. The hanging scroll in the *tokonoma* alcove is complemented by an arrangement of fresh flowers. Tea flowers are arranged as modestly and naturally as possible. On the second floor of the tearoom is a formal room with ten tatami mats. This guest room has walls of bold red ocher characteristic of this area, a *urushi* lacquered ceiling and ornate carvings on the transoms. These rooms, with their superb garden view over the veranda, are typical embodiments of the strong relationship between Japanese interiors and the garden.

The 18th owner, Michiko Mimou, learned the art of tea ceremony in her childhood. She has also inherited a vast collection of hanging scrolls, folding screens, tea utensils and pottery, from which she carefully selects items for display according to seasonal themes. Michiko says that on a fine day, when she is sitting quietly in the room with birds chirping and the leaves rustling in her garden, she feels the presence of her ancestors who must have done similar things in this very house.

Above: Mastering the tea ceremony involves learning five arts: tea preparation, ikebana, tea-style cooking, tearoom design and calligraphy. An elegant collection of calligraphy tools displayed on a platform (*biwa doko*) was originally meant for holding a four-stringed Japanese lute called a *biwa*. Here the *biwa doko* is acting as a *shoin* desk in formal rooms, on which it is customary to display writing tools—such desks were once used by monks for writing. A traditional ink stone is flanked by an ink-stick, and a brush that sits on a metal brush-rest shaped like a little boy. A tiny celadon water bottle, used for mixing ink, sits against a tiny blue–white screen.

Left: A symphony of color and simple lines lends the crucial sense of calm to this tearoom. Hand-crafted square cushions (*zabuton*) with persimmon dyes and a black lacquer container with sweets for a tea ceremony await guests. When the preparations for the tea ceremony are complete, the gong hanging from the ceiling on the left is struck, alerting guests in the next room that the preparations for the ceremony have been completed. Paper cut in an angular pattern lines the lowermost portion of the wall (*koshibari*), protecting the guests' kimonos from the brown clay.

Above: The square piece of tatami mat covers a hearth used for making tea during the winter season. Beautiful tea utensils have been set in front of an antique low screen. The iron teapot is an heirloom inscribed with the crest of an Edo Period local lord. The 16th century ceramic container with a goldfish design is from Jingdezhen in China.

Right: In the words of the famous tea master Sen no Rikyu, a delicious cup of tea should be served so that it is cooling in summer and warming in winter. Whipped green tea (*matcha*) is served here with a tea sweet in the color and shape of hydrangea, a seasonal flower.

This tearoom, known as Shika-no-ma, was built in the early 20th century. The distinctive feature of the room—named after the *shika*, or deer—is the delightful *fusuma* doors showing a pair of deer on a silver background. The painting depicts a buck looking down lovingly at a pregnant doe.

Above: The large stepping-stone is placed in front of the Shika-no-ma tearoom, indicating the separation of the interior and the exterior.

Right: Plants in a Japanese tea garden are selected to mimic natural growth as closely as possible, with just a few flowering plants. The moss-covered lantern in this garden is placed so as to be partially hidden by the foliage and not be overtly showy.

Above: Guests are ushered into this drawing room to eat a simple meal served before a ceremonial tea. A low folding screen (*byobu*) depicts a bamboo grove and the transom (*ranma*) above showcases openwork with a pattern of seven Chinese wise men in a bamboo forest.

Right: The *shoin* or the built-in desk on the left of the *tokonoma* marks this as a formal room. The bold red tone of its *tokonoma* wall is a special feature of the Kaga/Kanazawa area. Wood is first painted with red ocher, and then lacquered to a lustrous finish. The avoidance of repetition is a distinctive feature of the Sukiya style, as seen in the three different designs on the *shoji* in this room.

The relationship of the interior and the garden is very important in Sukiya-style architecture. The packed gravel floor inside extends out, strengthening the feeling of continuity. As is typical of homes in northern Japan, this *do-en* can be closed off with removable shutters, separating the columns from the garden, to provide an additional layer of protection against the winter cold. This garden contains the essential elements of a traditional tea garden (*cha-niwa*): the washbasin for purification, the stone lantern, a stepping-stone pathway, and the tree trunk and ground covered with ten kinds of moss.

A Celebration of Lacquer Craft

Lacquerware, also known as *shikki*, is a highly developed art in Japan. Obtained from the sap of the lacquer tree, lacquer (*urushi*) is used not only for decoration, but also for waterproofing and protecting wooden objects against moths and decay. Creating *shikki* is a laborious process in which 20 to 30 coats of various kinds of lacquer are applied onto a prepared wooden surface by hand. Each layer is left to dry in a moist, warm place for about a week before the next coat can be applied. The product is then polished with charcoal to enhance its luster and translucence.

Wajima City, the location of the Nakamuro house, has been famous for producing refined lacquerware for at least 500 years. Situated at the northern end of the Noto Peninsula facing the Japan Sea, Wajima was once a major port. The chiefs of lacquerware producers, called *nushi*, traveled from there by boat to trade with wealthy merchants and farmers around the country. In the golden age of the lacquer industry, lacquer guilds exchanged information about customers, helped improve techniques through friendly rivalries, and cultivated the *nushi* culture. The Nakamuro house was built by the head of one such guild in the days gone by, and has recently been restored by a modern *nushi*, Katsuro Nakamuro, the current owner of the house.

Nakamuro is the president of Wajimaya Honten, a long-established lacquerware company. When he found this house in 1988, it was over about 80 years old and was in a dilapidated state, having stood empty for years. Nakamuro felt that this house had a special historic aura, and was inspired to fulfill his dream of rebuilding *nushi* culture through renewing this house. He commissioned architect Shinji Takagi, who was born and lives in Wajima and is well versed in the use of regional material such as wood and lacquer, to help with his ambitious undertaking.

This elegant yet utilitarian building was originally built to serve as a guest house, a residence and a workplace, complete with an inner garden and a storehouse (*kura*), and a perimeter wall with a lacquered frame. Close inspection of the house revealed that its floors, ceilings, walls, verandas, posts and fixtures had all been lacquered using different techniques. Nakamuro set himself a challenge—the repaired and refurnished house had to exceed the original in terms of quality. During the renovation, new ideas were also incorporated, such as those in the design of lighting fixtures and a well. Elaborately carved and beautifully lacquered, the ornamental nail covers (*kugikakushi*) and door catches (*hikite*), as well as the decorative sliding doors added to the house are beautiful works of art in their own right.

With the renovations complete, this house once again represents the best of lacquer-based *nushi* culture. Nakamuro hopes that it will play an important role in passing on local culture and traditions to future generations.

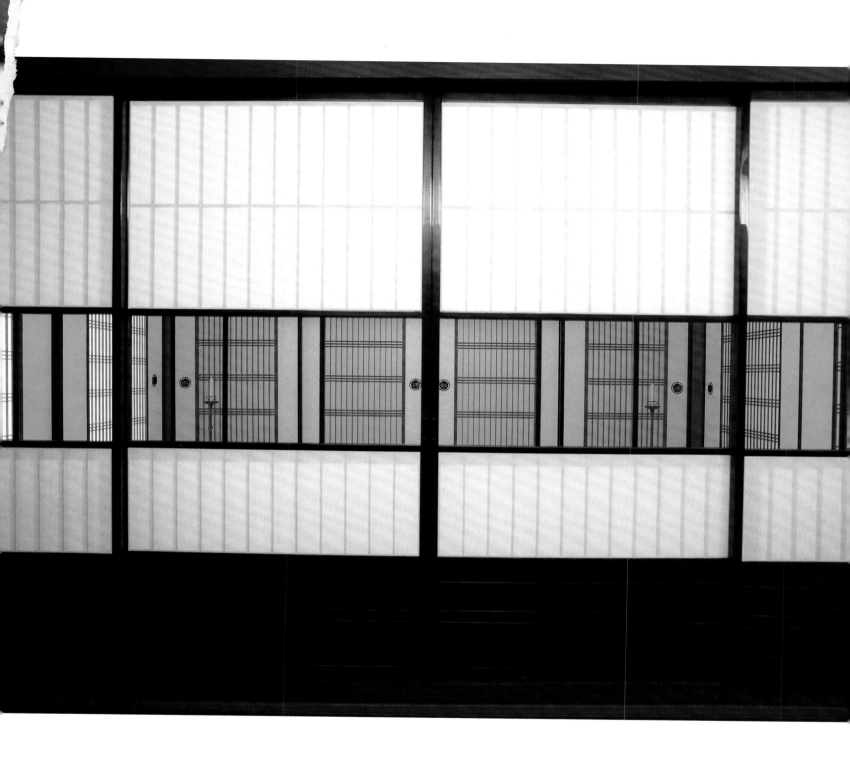

Above: *Shoji* doors serve as principal partitioning devices, in addition to providing a source of illumination and decoration. Here, *shoji* also control the view from the windows. The *fusuma* screens seen through the glass are special (*genji-fusuma*)—they have an inset of *shoji* in the center.

Left: The main earthen-floored corridor (*tori-niwa*) that connects the front and the back of the house, provides access to all the rooms. This photograph shows the entrances to the guest rooms and the Buddhist altar room on the left. The wood frame is made of *ate*, a locally grown conifer selected for its resistance to decay and its compatibility with lacquer. The wood has a special sheen resulting from the ten coats of lacquer that have been applied to it. The practical dark colors of this earth and sand floor replace the original flooring that was white in color, which must have been a challenge to maintain.

Above: Black lacquered wicker boxes such as these are art forms in themselves, and were used as light, portable trunks by the lacquer makers to carry their wares. Bowls in the foreground are of recent vintage, based on designs from books compiled in the Taisho Period (1912–1926).

Left: A lacquered tray is set for serving green tea and *yubeshi*, a noted confectionery of this district, made from aromatic citron and glutinous rice.

Opposite: These two tatami rooms adjoining the street were once used as reception rooms, where lacquerware producers (*nushi*) exchanged information after their long travels. A Buddhist altar can be seen in the background.

Above: The *fusuma* doors in the altar room have an unusual design with a lacquered board inset in the shape of a wild boar's eyes (*inome*).

Right: The painting on the lacquer boards depicts a mythical flower named *hosoge*, which is believed to bloom in the Buddha's paradise.

Opposite: The wooden lacquered veranda (*engawa*) and earthen-floored *doma* corridor form a buffer zone between the interior and the exterior of the house, designed here to respond to the weather conditions in this snowy district. Wooden doors (*amado*) enclose the *engawa* during the winter, expanding the living area, while in the summer the doors are stowed away to make the *engawa* an extension of the garden. The white plastered floor reflects the sunlight deep into the home's interiors.

Above: A four-stringed Japanese lute (*biwa*) stands beside the *tokonoma*, in keeping with the musical theme of the drawing room's decor.

Left top: The mythical flower *hosoge* adorns the lacquered door catch (*hikite*).

Left bottom: Gold inlay in the form of the Japanese lute decorates another door catch. Cropping a part of a picture to give a tantalizing idea of the whole is an old tradition in Japanese art.

Opposite: The 100-year-old lacquer dinner sets comprising matching bowls for rice, soup and other dishes are placed on footed trays.

Coming Home to an Old Machiya

Kyoto, the political and cultural center of Japan for more than a thousand years, is still the center of Japanese traditions in art and architecture. Besides the famous temples and shrines, Kyoto's architectural treasures include many *machiya* townhouses. Some of these date as far back as the Edo Period (1600–1868). Many were destroyed and damaged by fire and other disasters in the 1700s and 1800s, but were rebuilt in the Meiji or Taisho Periods. The townspeople who started the tradition of building these homes had neither the important titles nor the privileges of the aristocrats or the samurai of their time. Nevertheless, the houses that these people built incorporated beauty and function so well they continue to attract us today.

The *machiya* are usually located on lots averaging about five meters wide by about 20 meters deep, purposely kept narrow because property taxes were determined by the amount of street frontage. These homes usually had a shop or workroom in front, with private areas in the back. An earthen-floored long corridor, called a *tori-niwa*, extends from the entrance all the way to the back of the house providing access to all the rooms. There may also be another earthen floor area called a *doma*, reserved for cooking or other chores. Other rooms are raised on a plinth, and people are expected to remove their shoes before entering. Honored guests or customers may be ushered to a more formal room in the central part of the house, located next to a tiny elegant garden (*tsubo-niwa* or *senzai*) that brings light and air to the adjoining rooms. Formal rooms are often decorated with fine woods, coffered ceilings, as well as some elements of the aristocratic Shoin style.

Architect Toru Baba and his wife, essayist Keiko Asou, had always wanted to live in a *machiya*, but were having a great deal of trouble finding one. Traditional houses in Japan are hard to find, as they are increasingly being demolished by owners opting for modern conveniences and low maintenance. Contributing to this ongoing loss is the lack of public support for preserving buildings that are not designated cultural properties. Toru and Keiko were finally able to find this wonderful *machiya*, a former retreat for a merchant family in the early Showa Period (1926–1989). As it had been unoccupied for years, this home required extensive renovations, including the cleaning and refinishing of walls and floorboards. These surfaces were lacquered by this energetic young couple themselves. The new owners have also added several unusual and personal elements to the house, making this *machiya* truly their own.

It is quite difficult to equip a small *machiya* with modern conveniences such as air-conditioning and heating. Instead of worrying about making these changes, Toru and Keiko have decided to endure periods of intense heat and cold in order to stay in touch with the changing seasons, which is more in keeping with how they wish to live their lives. Throughout the year, the couple also enjoy the local events and festivals that take place outside their front door—another advantage of living in a *machiya*.

Above. Toru and Keiko have kept the furnishings to a minimum and the décor of their small townhouse as simple as possible, thus giving it a feeling of spaciousness. Here, camellia buds, are arranged in a simple bud vase placed atop a *tansu* chest. Camellia flowers were not used in ikebana arrangements in the past, because the falling off of the ripe blossom from its stem was associated with the beheading of a samurai.

Right: The hanging flowerpot in the entrance hall holds an inviting arrangement of magnolias, seen here from the tearoom through the arched door called *katoh-guchi*. The present owners installed the wall on the left with two round windows to replace an old sliding partition. The bamboo and reed grid in these openings, called *shitaji mado*, is created by leaving the lattice framework of the walls unplastered, providing a rustic touch. The ochre color of the walls comes from natural clay called *osaka-tsuchi*, which had been also used in the original interior of this house.

Above: This room is cozy and warm in winter. The walls are finished with fine orange sand. The lower part of the walls is covered with rice paper (*koshibari*), traditionally installed to protect kimonos from the mud walls, but used here to reflect the daylight to brighten the room.

Left: Subdued colors and a system of simple lines lend order to Japanese interiors. The very small three-mat sitting area, furnished with a low table and small reed cushions, is seen here through an open, single-panel screen (*tsuitate*).

Above: This simple but elegant entrance is for guests. Japanese craftsmen take pride in making the *shoji* latticework. Although very thin, it does not warp over time. This is achieved by using wood with a straight, parallel grain, taken from the center of *hinoki* (Japanese cypress) trees.

Right: Another unusual detail in the house is this backlit white glass floor of the small *tokonoma* alcove (90 x 90 centimeters) in the drawing room (*zashiki*). The walls of the *tokonoma* are pasted with thick sculpted paper, to which persimmon tannin has been applied.

Top: The earthen-floored kitchen is located in a *tori-niwa*, which also serves as the main corridor of the house. The kitchen is open to the sky, letting sunlight in and smoke and heat out through the roof beams. Over the years, these rafters have become soot-covered, and are an impressive sight. This type of terrazzo sink (*jintogi*) is rarely found today, even in Kyoto and other traditional areas of Japan.

Above: Traditional wooden shelves in the kitchen were replaced by contemporary glass shelving for storing dishware and seasonings.

Left: An earthen-floored room called a *doma* is traditionally the place for cooking, craft work and other informal activities in a *machiya*. Here, a tatami room has been remodeled into an earthen-floored dining room. The original floors in the foreground also were previously covered with tatami mats, but have now been replaced with wooden floorboards. The new owners applied several layers of lacquer to the floors so that they harmonize with the rest of the house.

Antiques Find a New Home in an Old Minka

The unassuming beauty of Japan's *minka* farmhouses comes from the use of natural building materials and traditional techniques perfected over hundreds of years. The word *minka* originally meant a home of a common person who was not an aristocrat or a samurai. However, it is now primarily used to describe farmhouses with heavy wooden structures and thatched roofs. These buildings also illustrate a deep understanding and appreciation of wood in Japan. The love of nature instilled by Japan's ancient religious beliefs, an abundance of forests, and a damp climate have contributed to wood becoming the preferred building material for over a thousand years. Since common people did not have access to fine straight woods and quality cutting devices, *minka* often exploit the beauty of large uncut timbers in their natural form. These timbers are rendered shiny and dark over time by soot from the large hearth that was the core of life for the large families that lived and worked in these homes. Instead of chimneys, the smoke in such homes escaped through the thatch, moth-proofing the wood at the same time.

The *minka* now owned by graphic designer Takeshi Yamamoto is located in Keihoku Town, an hour's drive south of central Kyoto. The home is situated among mountains and valleys where cedar trees called *kitayama-sugi* rise straight into the sky. These trees have been carefully cultivated for centuries to provide the flawless straight, fine-grained wood used for sophisticated Sukiya-style structures.

Yamamoto had originally bought the *minka* in an attempt to preserve it. He heard from a wood-artist friend that a nearby *minka* of fine wood was to going be demolished so that the land could be sold. The story deeply moved Yamamoto and his wife—who had developed a keen appreciation for *minka*—and they decided to purchase the structure in 1995. They initially planned to use the *minka* for weekends only, with a view of settling down in it permanently in the future. While inspecting the house, Yamamotos discovered the construction plaque (*munafuda*) placed on the ridgepole, which confirmed that a skilled master carpenter had built the house in 1912. A watercourse circled the premises, which also has a solid rammed-earth boundary wall built on a stone base. The Yamamotos decided to leave the structure and the exterior of this handsome house just as they found it, simply re-tiling the roof and refinishing the stucco walls. However, more remodeling was ultimately needed in the interior to make it suitable for a modern lifestyle. Using instincts and expert advice, they removed many of the later additions and ill-matched fixtures that were not in the spirit of the original house. They replaced these with old fittings and tatami mats purchased from demolition sites of old *machiya* in Kyoto. After consultation with a lacquer expert, fresh raw lacquer was applied to the floorboards.

The Yamamotos have filled their new home with antiques lovingly collected over many years from antique markets and demolition sites throughout Kyoto. Their collection includes pottery, lacquerware, glassware, ornamental hairpins (*kanzashi*), furniture, lighting fixtures and *fusuma* doors with beautiful paintings. Infused with the Yamamoto's love for their home, new life is given to these old treasures.

Above: Takeshi Yamamoto has collected antiques since he was in his 20s. These blue and white dishes are some of his favorite porcelain collection pieces. Eye-catching fluted Imari has been produced in Kyushu since the Momoyama Period (1572–1603), when this style was brought to Japan from Korea during the pottery wars. Blue and white pottery has also constituted an important portion of Japan exports throughout history, with rough and rejected pieces used as ships' ballast.

Left: The water laver (*chozu-bachi*) seen through the window is a type used as an accent in gardens, and was originally used for washing hands.

Opposite: The wood-floored living room, tatami room and the veranda spaces flow around the central pillar in this restored *minka*. Bamboo blinds called *sudare*, traditionally used on windows during summer, are used here to provide visual definition to one part of the room without disturbing the flow of space.

Above: The crescent-shaped hanging vase bearing a camellia creates a nice silhouette against the *shoji* screen. Hairpins (*kanzashi*) with ornamental heads are a popular collector's item, and are displayed here next to a lacquered box.

Left: The sliding partitioning system in Japanese homes skillfully expands or contracts space according to need. In the front room, a tobacco tray with a fire pan and an ashtray sit beside a square cushion (*zabuton*). The room at the back with the *tokonoma* is for formal use.

Above: Made since the Edo Period (1600–1867),
Japanese chests (*tansu*) derive their beauty from
a practical but tasteful mix of hard and soft woods
and decorative hardware. Hardwood is used for
the framework, while the softwood used for the
drawers and shelves keeps the contents ventilated
and, at the same time, is light enough so that the
tansu can be moved easily. A pair of porcelain
guardian dogs (*shishi*) sit atop this simple *tansu*,
displayed in front of calligraphy screens.

Left: This folding screen with a depiction of a
multi-petaled cherry tree on a golden background
was made from *fusuma* doors originally painted
in the mid-18th century. Such *fusuma* and *byobu*
were designed for lighting with papered lamps
(*andon*)—a method of lighting that still produces a
deeply satisfying effect.

This wood-floored room is a remodeled tatami room. Yamamoto had painstakingly applied layer after layer of lacquer to the floor himself. The family collection of pottery and glassware is at home here. The chest shown in the background is known as a *kuruma-dansu*, and was made during the end of the Edo Period (1600–1867). It has built-in wheels, which allows it to be easily rolled out of danger in the event of fire.

Above: The use of horizontal and vertical lines combined with muted shades form the aesthetic basis of traditional Japanese architecture. This earthen-floored corridor connects the front and the back of the house.

Left: This lower level, earthen-floored space (*doma*) was originally meant to serve as both a kitchen and a workshop, and still retains a wood-fired cooking stove. The curved beam on the rear wall shows an example of the rough timbers often used in *minka*.

Right: A particularly unique bath (*goemon-buro*) is surrounded by blue and white tiles imprinted with a popular early 20th century design. Rarely seen today, this type of bath has a metal tub heated from beneath by an external wood-fueled stove. The lid leaning against the wall is placed over the tub to keep the water warm. A wooden panel is pushed onto the floor, providing an insulated surface to sit on and protecting bathers from the hot metal.

A House with a Cosmopolitan Interior

Japan ended its self-imposed isolation in 1868 with the Meiji Revolution, and soon emerged as a leader in silk trade due to the techniques in dying and weaving that had been developed over its long history. The Kawabata house was built 120 years ago in the middle of the Meiji Era (1868–1912) by Mr Kawabata, a silk merchant who had made his fortune by exporting Japanese silk from Yokohama, one of the first ports to be opened to foreign trade. With an estate of over a million square meters, Kawabata was one of the biggest landowners in this part of Gunma Prefecture, not far from Tokyo. This remarkable man had also served as the village chief since the tender age of 17, and later governed a vast domain as a squire. As befitting his status, Kawabata built an imposing two-storied wooden house in Fujioka City amid mulberry fields where silkworms were raised. Built with the choicest materials —selected after much care and consideration—this house took almost ten years to complete. Legend has it that the amount of wood deemed inferior and thus discarded during the construction process would have been enough to build yet another house.

Nestled among age-old willow trees, the grounds of the house also includes seven storehouses (*kura*) for stocking rice and fermented soybean paste (*miso*), a majestic boundary wall with several gates, and other small buildings. The estate is so impressive that the Ministry of Education in Japan has designated 19 of the structures on the compound as Registered Tangible Cultural Properties of Japan.

This 300-square-meter house on this very large estate is now owned and lovingly taken care of by Yoshiko Tsai, the great-granddaughter of the builder. It is quite unusual in Japan for this large a property to stay in a family over several generations due to the very high inheritance taxes in Japan. Yoshiko managed to inherit it from her mother only because of the special efforts made by her ancestors to keep the property in the family. She and her husband Jaw Shen Tsai, a Chinese–American physicist, use it as a vacation home on their frequent visits from Tokyo.

Yoshiko feels that although the Japanese are quite comfortable removing their shoes outside the house and living on tatami matted rooms without chairs, it was difficult for her husband and their foreign guests to enjoy the house in this manner. She also believes that the usual Western furniture looks inappropriate in a traditional Japanese home, but that the lines of Chinese furniture and Western antiques are quite suitable for it. Unlike the Japanese, the Chinese have a long tradition of sitting on chairs and have developed their own style of furniture with linear beauty. Thus Yoshiko, who studied interior design when she was in New York, redecorated her family home by adding Chinese furniture and other comforts to it. The new furniture in the house includes several pieces which Yoshiko bought from Shanghai—these pieces now happily co-exist with the ancestral furnishings in her home. As a result of her talent and efforts, the interior of this historic house now showcases an international flair well suited to its modern use.

Above: Visitors are greeted at the entrance (*genkan*) by an arrangement of fresh flowers. A single-panel gold screen (*tsuitate*) dresses up the *genkan* and provides privacy to the interior. The frames of the *shoji* screen have been made with black lacquered wood. Such frames are found only in very formal rooms, while unpainted wooden frames are the norm in more casual interiors.

Left: All *shoji* and *fusuma* doors have been opened to allow the breeze in during good weather, providing a clear view from the *genkan* all the way to the garden at the back of the house.

Above: These *shoji* doors with intricate patterns were made by very skilled craftsmen over several years. The delicate frames are fashioned from the straight-grained, warp-resistant central portion of tree trunks with even growth rings.

Left: This folding screen (*byobu*) with calligraphic work is an heirloom which now finds its place behind the white lily that elegantly announces the arrival of summer. The traditional *byobu* use special paper hinges that allow the front as well as the back of the screens to be used. Chinese furniture from Shanghai complements the Japanesque atmosphere. A sitting room with Chinese furniture can be seen through the open *fusuma* doors.

Above: Designed as a display platform, the base of the *tokonoma* alcove is usually raised one step above the floor level. One side of the *tokonoma* is supported by the *toko-bashira* post. Here the *toko-bashira* is made of natural black persimmon wood. The white colors of the *kakejiku* scroll and other decorations reveal Yoshiko's sensitivity to the dark finish of the *tokonoma* walls.

Right: A blend of East and West, this high table and the antique chairs from England sit in front of a Chinese scroll painting.

Above: The veranda overlooking the garden serves as an informal place in which family members relax or entertain friends. Perched in a corner, a bamboo basket bearing chrysanthemums of various colors is softly lit by daylight coming through the *shoji*.

Right: Yoshiko's taste is evident in her collection of animal objects. The lacquered wooden cow sitting in front of the cupboard was the first antique she ever bought. A pheasant-shaped incense burner (*koro*) rests on the middle shelf of the cupboard.

Opposite: Yoshiko's collection of favorite things includes a Chinese-style bamboo birdcage, a Japanese doll and tableware pottery.

Overleaf: A small three-mat dressing room feels expansive as it is filled with soft light coming through the *shoji*. Movable sections within *shoji* windows allow the user of this room to control their view. The shadows of the *shoji* frame form a decorative pattern on the floor, which changes as the sun moves across the horizon.

A Potter Meets His Minka

Tucked away in a bamboo grove and rice fields in Tanba Town near Kyoto, this farmhouse (*minka*) looks like the backdrop of a tale from old Japan. The lichen-covered thatched roof and the earthen walls of the *minka* blend so well into the landscape that is hard to imagine that this huge structure was brought here as recently as 1994 from its original location east of Lake Biwa. Now this 135-year-old *minka* is the home and atelier of potter Naoto Ishii and his wife. This new site for the house was chosen after careful consideration of wind directions and atmospheric pressure, because Ishii also wanted to fulfill his long-cherished dream of building a climbing kiln (*noborigama*) of the type that has been used in Japan since the Middle Ages. This type of kiln consists of several linked chambers built into a hillside, with the opening for fire kindling in the lowest section, and the chimney at the top. Most potters in Japan do not use this sort of a kiln because it is nearly impossible to control it due to the various forces of nature at work inside. However, this is exactly the aspect of working with a *noborigama* that fascinates Ishii, who points to his work saying, "Who made this pottery? Was it really I?"

Architect Katsumi Yasuda, an old friend of Ishii's, is quite knowledgeable about traditional homes. He believes that an architect should not impose his own ideas on his clients, but should instead facilitate the creation of a space that expresses the client's spirit. Yasuda found Ishii's *minka*, which had originally belonged to a wheat farmer, and had been thatched over with wheat straw. He advised Ishii during the taking of measurements, labeling, dismantling, transfer of the house piece-by-piece to the new plot, and its reconstruction. The basic composition of the house was maintained, but certain features such as a staircase and windows were added to improve its circulation and ventilation. Old fixtures were reused where possible, and the roof of the house was re-thatched with rice straw. Using traditional techniques, the walls were filled-in with wattle made of split bamboo lattice tied with rice-straw rope, and then daubed with mud. The inside walls were plastered with iron-rich mud brought from a nearby bamboo forest. The iron in this mud resulted in rust spots on the walls, making them all the more charming.

Deep awe and respect for nature form the essential starting point of Japanese arts, especially pottery. When he recently climbed Mount Asama, an active volcano, Ishii was struck by the beauty of the countless rocks formed, colored and fired by volcanic eruptions, as if by God, the potter. This experience inspired him to create things that are stirring or forceful in their own way.

Ishii is dedicated to the primitive processes of making folk-style pottery, particularly Richo, a style popular during the Korean Joseon Dynasty (1392–1910). He works the mud and clod with his hands, squeezing it through his fingers, and fires the shaped clay with special firewood in his *noborigama*—this involves burning wood continually for four-and-a-half days. Ishii spends most of his day in his studio. He takes time off for meals with his wife, to walk his dog, and to occasionally drink sake with his friends. He fires his *noborigama* once a year. He feels as if the age-old *minka* has helped slow down time for him.

Above right: Ishii crafts a wide range of pottery in this studio, ranging from vases and tableware to decorative objects. Here, the potter's wheel and the tools of his trade enjoy a moment of rest, covered with clay dust.

Above left: The black lacquered wooden rice chest is of the type used in a feudal lord's (*daimyo*) procession in the Edo Period (1600–1867). It was carried on shoulder poles inserted through the side handles. A bowl made by Ishii is displayed here, holding moss and grass from the garden.

Left: A creation by the potter hangs above a rustic Korean chest. The heavy wooden object, which Ishii now uses to grind clay, is actually an old Korean mortar originally used to pound steamed rice into cakes for New Year's Day.

Above: A traditional Japanese-style built-in hearth located in the middle of a room allows people to gather around it, sharing their warmth and a sense of intimacy, unobstructed by furniture.

Left: Tatami mats (*ryukyu-datami*) of the type originally produced in Okinawa, the southernmost island of Japan, are rougher and stronger than those made of *igusa* grass, which is the usual material used for making mats. These mats also have a special aesthetic effect on the room where they are used as they do not have the usual cloth border. A chest for books is seen in the background, built in Ishii's favorite style—Richo.

Opposite: Traditionally, meals in a *minka* home were eaten around the large hearth (*irori*) that formed the focal point of family life. In its new incarnation, this *minka* also has a Western-style dining room. The dining table has been made from boards left over from assembling the wooden floor.

An Old Farmhouse Gears up for the Future

Minka, the traditional farmhouses of Japan, are a wonderful but fast disappearing building genre. They are generally constructed of heavy and often uneven timbers, bamboos, thatched roof and mud walls. *Minka* that have survived today were built by wealthy farmers and merchants, and represent the ingenuity of the Japanese folk craft traditions.

In spite of their charm, *minka* are often dark and cold, lack modern conveniences, and are very expensive to re-thatch and maintain. For these reasons, the number of these houses had been dwindling till quite recently. However, there is now a renewed interest in these homes from several people who are working toward saving and restoring them. In the tradition of the well known German architect Bruno Taut before him, Karl Bengs, another German architect, has, over the past 20 years, become an important representative for this small group of people. One of the 180-year-old *minka* he has saved is now his own home, located in Matsudai Town, one of the heaviest snowfall area in the mountainous interior of Niigata Prefecture. This region also produces premier rice called *koshi-hikari*, cultivated in the traditional way, which provides the straw used for thatching this and other houses in this area.

Disassembling and reassembling *minka* is a relatively simple process due to the remarkable method of construction used by traditional Japanese carpenters. An elaborate system of mortise and tenon joints is constructed in advance, and then the timbers raised and fitted to form a frame without any metal fittings and adhesives. Bengs' house was reconstructed in this way. Making wooden joints is a recognized and respected art in Japan. On this main frame, a lighter frame of bamboo is constructed using bamboos and ropes, and a 50-centimeter thick thatch roof is applied. The details of the house and its finishing were painstakingly restored using traditional methods, and 20th century comforts added without compromising its integrity. These additions included insulating materials, double-glazed windows, floor heating, a modern kitchen and bathrooms. In addition, balustrades, fixtures and door-knobs from other old houses or antique shops have been added to complement the rustic beauty of the house. Bengs himself applied stucco to some parts of the walls. However, taking the liberty of being a foreigner in Japan, Bengs has painted the plastered parts of the exterior of this house a light pink, a color not usually associated with *minka*.

Besides his own home, Bengs has helped save and restore several other pre-modern buildings in Japan. Bengs is now working toward creating a "village" in Niigata, where *minka* from all parts of Japan may be restored and reconstructed, so that people from all regions can use them as vacation homes. Such restorations by Bengs and others are helping the Japanese people appreciate afresh the beauty of their old buildings, as well as highlight the sustainable lifestyle of old Japan, which was in complete harmony with nature.

Above: *Minka* derive their beauty from the stateliness of heavy timber and other natural materials used in a manner perfected over centuries. The lustrous patina on the wood comes from years of smoke from the hearth. A loft or a second floor in *minka* was traditionally used only for raising silkworms or for storage. Here it has been remodeled into living quarters with the addition of a staircase. The handrail was bought at an antique shop, and had been originally designed to be used horizontally.

Right: Roughhewn beech beams positioned to emphasize the beauty of their natural curve, and polished zelkova posts were connected together with notched joints when the house was originally constructed 180 years ago. This made it relatively easy to reassemble this *minka* in its new location.

This room contains a square, open hearth (*irori*), which was once the center of family life in a farmhouse, providing heat, light and a place to cook. During the renovation of the house, Bengs added large double-glazed windows to this room, giving it a more open atmosphere. These windows were imported from Germany because of their high insulation quality.

Above left: Staircases were rare in traditional Japanese architecture. Instead, a step-chest (*kaidandansu*) was used to provide access to upper floors. Removable drawers and a closet under the steps provided the much needed storage space in a traditional house. These chests are unique to Japan and a popular item with antique furniture collectors.

Above right: The corner of the loft serves as Bengs' workplace, from where he has a good view of the surrounding countryside.

Left: Unfinished logs and bamboo bound with rice-straw rope hold the house together, and impart a rugged beauty to it, made apparent with the addition of electric lights in this area that has traditionally been dark. Simple white walls accentuate the earthy textures of the beams and reeds on the ceiling. A lantern of the type used as an accent in gardens has been attached here to the stair post for providing light to the bedroom.

A Home in Snow Country

Koichi Sato is the 11th head of a family of landowners in Oomagari City, Akita Prefecture, located near the Japan Sea in the northern part of Honshu, the main island of Japan. Winters here are severe, and everything mantles over with thick snow from November to April, presenting a beautiful sight on moonlit nights. Scarlet-tinged autumn leaves herald the coming of the long winter, prompting local people to set about winter-proofing their homes. The traditional houses here are wrapped with boards and rice straw mats (*mushiro*) to protect glass windows and doors from snow falling off roofs. This makes the interior of the homes dim for months on end, while the outdoors are bright with snow. Removing snow from their roofs and entrances is part of the daily routine of life in Oomagari City.

The Sato house was built in 1894 in this harsh countryside. While the exterior and parts of this imposing edifice are built to withstand extreme weather conditions, parts of the interior have been designed in the delicate aristocratic Shoin style. A wooden fence (*itabei*) made of scorched planks of Japanese cedar lines the approach to the Sato house and extends seemingly endlessly. The house is hidden from view from the main gate (*mon*). A stone pavement runs from the *mon* to the central gate in the second boundary wall, where one gets the first full view of this majestic two-storey house surrounded by aged cedar trees. Shoin-style houses were considered a privilege of the samurai class during the 15th century, but had become an acceptable style for people like village headmen and wealthy merchants or farmers toward the end of the Edo Period (1600–1867). In the years after the Meiji Revolution, such houses continued to speak of the status and sophistication of the owner. The front entrance of this house is used only for ceremonial occasions such as weddings or funerals, while family members normally use a smaller door on the side of the house. In addition to the main house, this vast estate includes some fireproof storehouses (*kura*), a Shinto shrine, several ancestral tombs, and wooded hills, which were the source of firewood and charcoal before electricity or gas became available.

The Sato house took ten years to build and was completed in 1894 by the eighth head of the family. The fact that the house has needed very few repairs for nearly a hundred years and is still in very good condition is a testament to the skill of the craftsmen from the neighboring villages who built it. High-quality woods such as cedar, Japanese cypress, pine, and zelkova were used in the construction of this house. The loving care shown by its inhabitants is also remarkable, as it speaks for their love of traditions and their family history. The house is cold in winter and hard to maintain, but the Satos are intent on keeping it in the family as a symbol of honor to their ancestors.

Above: This ceremonial outer gate is in the shape of a warrior's helmet, and is roofed over with ceramic tiles. Such gates were symbolic of the status and sophistication of the owner.

Left: This inner wall is of the type usually seen in samurai villas or temples, and is made of scorched pine planks, *sikkui* plaster and tiles. The understated beauty of this wall leading to the inner gate is augmented here by the autumn colors of gingko and maple trees that grow alongside it.

Previous pages: The heavy roof and deep overhangs are an aesthetically important part of a traditional Japanese home. This roof is covered with ceramic tiles, which were unusual in this area where most homes used to be roofed with thatch. The serene dignity of this house is enhanced by the vast garden of ancient cedar trees around it. The left wing of the house holds the formal drawing room, while the entrance is located in the right wing.

Left: The formal drawing room with 24 tatami mats and a high ceiling is made in aristocratic Shoin style, so named after a ceremonial built-in desk of the type seen below the window. The oversized decorative alcove (*tokonoma*) is in keeping with the impressive size of this room. The suitably large hanging screen (*kakejiku*) displayed in it was painted by Hoan Kosugi, a famous artist. The walls are plastered with a unique plaster of fine sand. *Fusuma* doors are decorated with real gold and silver dust. The lacquered (*urushi*) frames of the *shoji* screens, the exquisite ornamental nail covers (*kugi-kakushi*) and door handles (*hikite*) are a sign of rare luxury.

Above: The antique pieces displayed on this open shelf are from the collection of Sato's grandfather, who had served as the village chief for about 20 years till he was in his 50s.

Right: This door handle (*hikite*) has an elaborate flower pattern of open metal work and lacquer.

Opposite: The window and the open door bring the beauty of the garden into this grand reception room that is used on formal occasions. With the *fusuma* partitions removed, the 18-mat room and the 24-mat room can be combined to seat 40 diners.

The wide veranda (*engawa*) has been lacquered to protect the wood floor from rain. Fifteen sliding storm shutters (*amado*) can be taken out of their closet (*to-bukuro*) located at the end of the veranda, and pulled into the rails just outside the posts on the garden side. This is done to protect the large drawing room from cold, rain and snow. Constructed more than a hundred years ago, the *amado* have not warped and can still be easily pushed one after another, like a train of cars along the rails.

Above: The wooden brazier (*hako-hibachi*) is used for warmth and for boiling water for green tea. Charcoal is arranged in the center under a trivet provided to support an iron kettle.

Left: The Satos enjoy fresh produce from their estate. The big bamboo colander has persimmons and gourds picked in the garden. The small colander has chestnuts gathered in nearby woods. The edible pink chrysanthemums in the basket at the back are the special flower of this area, and make a pretty garnish on Japanese dishes, meant to please the eye as well as the palate.

Opposite: The small dressing table, the low towel rack and the tiny lamp (*andon*) furnish this dressing room that is used by guests while seated on the tatami mats. Such décor is reminiscent of classical Japanese inns.

A Sukiya-style Setting for an Art Gallery

Located in the central part of Japan, Tajimi City in Gifu Prefecture is well known for its Mino pottery. In this city, Masanobu Ando, an artist from a family of pottery wholesalers, has created a dramatic gallery called Galerie Momogusa, which is housed in an equally dramatic Sukiya-style building. Built in 1896, this house with its delicate timber and an exquisite interior was originally owned by a doctor in Nagoya and was slated for demolition when Ando saw it and decided to purchase it for his gallery. After reconstruction, the house forms a fitting backdrop for this talented potter's collection of beautiful ceramics and other objects.

Although every room in this house is made of wood, tatami mats and *shoji* doors, each room has a different character. The earthen floor and eight-tatami room adjoining the porch (*genkan*) is meant for relaxation and is used for the family's daily activities. In contrast, the ten-mat drawing room (*zashiki*) and the ten-tatami anteroom in the innermost part of the house are very formal and meant for receiving guests. A six-tatami room and a Buddhist altar separate these two parts of the house. This central area has an air of sacredness, quite distinct from the other parts. Ando considered the character of each room as well as seasons and annual events while designing the interiors of this house.

Ando's displays are simple yet dramatic. A serpentine line of wooden boards bearing art objects runs throughout the house, from the earthen floor to the back rooms. The boards were originally meant for making sturdy paper stencils (*ise-katagami*) with intricate patterns for printing kimono fabrics. The line intentionally culminates in front of a hanging scroll (*kakejiku*) at the alcove (*tokonoma*) in the innermost room. Although hanging scrolls usually have paintings or calligraphic work on them, this particular one made by Ando himself is simply a composition of white paper. To Ando, this work signifies a void or inanity (*ku*). This concept comes from the Zen verse "*shiki-soku-ze-ku*," which means, "all is vanity" or "every form in reality is empty." Ando also enjoys experimenting with the subtle nuances that the placement of simple objects and light can convey about the accessibility or sacredness of spaces. Large pieces of art are displayed with stage-like lighting, while the empty spaces around them amplify their presence.

Ando unites the Eastern and Western influences in his life in Galerie Momogusa. While he was busy creating European-style contemporary art in his 20s, he began to wonder if he did in fact have a cultural or ethnic identity as a Japanese. In order to understand himself better, he took up the study of ceremonial tea (*chanoyu*) just before he turned 30. Twenty years later, Ando feels that he has been imbued with the spirit of the tea ceremony, which for him consists of attaining an intuitive and open state of mind. He feels that he can now appreciate works of art simply for what they are, with a clear perception, unhindered by thoughts about their background. With this attitude as his starting point, his exhibits include things regardless of whether they are Japanese or Western, old or new.

Ando created this large art object using rolled up corrugated cardboard. He believes that its location gives the elevated space a feeling of sacredness similar to a *kekkai*, an unseen barrier that demarcated hallowed places in ancient Japan. Its positioning also gives it the role of separating the secular world in front of it from the sacred world behind it. Special tatami mats without cloth borders (*ryukyu-datami*) have been used in this interior. These types of tatami mats are used for judo gyms or farmers' workshops because of their durability. They provide an element of informality to the spaces in which they are placed. The square lighting fixture was designed by Ando and custom made by a stained glass artist. The vertical and horizontal lines of the lamp as well as those of the structure emphasize the roundness of the art piece.

Above: A wooden door made of an intricate pattern of woven shingles (*ajiro*) partitions the hall. Individual shingles were torn off by a hatchet instead of being cut evenly with a saw, giving this door a special effect. A ceramic sculpture created by Keiji Ito, an artist admired by Ando, is displayed with dramatic lighting at the far end of the hall.

Left: A simple white ceramic art object, a large wooden dish, light and *shoji* screens have all been used to create a dramatic stage-like effect. Wooden boards like those that run through the house for display have been used here to subtly define the area beyond as inaccessible. This room had been previously used as a Buddhist altar.

The zigzag line of wooden display boards runs through the various rooms and comes to rest in front of the *tokonoma*. This line of boards is designed to remind guests of a meandering path in a tea garden, with the bowls of varying shapes reminiscent of stepping-stones. By removing the sliding doors, the 16-tatami anteroom and the drawing room have been combined to make a sizeable exhibition space.

Above: These bowls, made by Ando, are of the type used in tea ceremonies, and have been strategically placed on the zigzag line of display boards.

Left: Ando made the contemporary scroll hanging in the *tokonoma* using layers of white Japanese paper. The void in the center of the scroll is designed to represent "*ku*," a three-dimensional void. The tool hanging near the window is a wooden hammer used to ring the bell to announce the start of the tea ceremony.

An Old Parlor with an Old Tree

Located near the Japan Sea, Kanazawa is an old castle town that was well known during the Edo Period (1600–1867) for its flourishing economy as well as a culture that was quite distinct from Kyoto. The town's traditions have been well preserved, making it one of the favorite destinations for people who are interested in Japanese arts and culture. One building that is reminiscent of its gracious history is the Nakamura parlor, which shares its grounds with two modern buildings and a magnificent 400-year-old Japanese white pine tree.

The *fusuma* doors of this one-room parlor lead into a simple and serene interior. This eight-mat formal room with an *engawa* was built in the Sukiya style in 1933, and serves as both a drawing room and a tearoom. The late Baizan Nakamura, who built this room in his 20s, was a potter well known for making tea-ceremony utensils with beautiful and novel designs. The touch of the artist's ingenuity is evident in this simple room, achieved here without gorgeous materials or expensive features such as wooden posts and ceiling boards of precious wood, sculptured *ranma*, *fusuma* with gold detailing and other decorative elements. Severe discipline, with a spirit of playfulness is the quintessence of the Sukiya style ("tea style") in Japan, and the Nakamura parlor is a good example of that. An example of Sukiya-style playfulness is found in the sliding doors on a row of low closets, which are made of wood that was selected for its apparently moth-eaten texture. The room also has a fireplace (*ro*) sunk into the floor for tea-ceremony events. When not in use, it is covered with a board made by boldly contrasting rough weather-worn wood with smooth, fine-grained pine wood. A similar spirit is seen in the design of the door handles (*hikite*). The outside *hikite* have an image of an iron club representative of the devil, while those on the inside are engraved with a Chinese character for good luck. These door handles are a reference to the Japanese Bean-throwing festival in spring, during which people scatter soybeans throughout the house, shouting, "Out with the devil, in with good fortune." However, these details do not detract from the simple beauty of this room, which is in complete harmony with the natural elements of the garden outside, including the ancient pine tree.

Architect Hiroshi Naito helped reconstruct the Nakamura parlor in 1996, after it had been dismantled at the suggestion of Baizan himself. This parlor, along with the old family house, was taken down to make space for the new homes that Nakamura's sons were planning to build (one of these is featured on pages 214–223). Fortunately, the Nakamura family later decided to reconstruct this parlor in its original form exactly where it had been before, because it had a special place in their lives, and also because this exquisite room would be irreplaceable in the future. Baizan's three sons, Kinpei, Takuo and Kohei, are all potters and display their father's originality in their contemporary ceramics. Takuo says, "In my youth, I felt put off by this parlor because I thought it was ostentatious, but now I admit that growing up with it has helped develop my creativity."

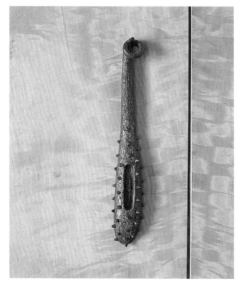

Top left: This door handle (*hikite*) is in the shape of the devil's iron club.

Above: The square ceramic container with a red lid was made by Baizan for serving broiled eel on rice —a special dish usually served in a lacquered box.

Right: The flower vase made by Baizan sits on the low closet. The doors of these closets have been made of apparently moth-eaten wood, selected for its special texture. The green and white door handles (*hikite*) were created by Baizan. The bell hanging from the ceiling is by Baizan's eldest son, Kinpei. His second son, Takuo, made the modern container seen in the foreground. Such containers are used during tea ceremonies to hold the water for rinsing cups.

Bottom left: The sunken stone fireplace (*ro*) located in the middle of the room is used for tea ceremonies in winter. Its unusual cover is fashioned from a jux-taposition of smooth pine and seasoned wood.

The flower arrangement in this vase by Baizan is a creation of 93-year-old Mrs Nakamura. Placing a mat under the vase gives the arrangement its own space. The walls seen through the open *shoji* are glazed with red ocher, an architectural accent typical of Kanazawa. The simple paper lantern hanging above was designed by Isamu Noguchi. The round light fixture accentuates the horizontal and vertical lines of the room. *Hikite* on the *fusuma* door are fashioned in the shape of a white egret.

Above: This small parlor is now positioned between two modern additions to the property. Standing next to the ancient tree and surrounded by a moss-covered garden, it looks very dignified.

Left: The 400-year-old Japanese white pine stands in the center of the garden like a guardian of the old house, controlling the flow of light into the room. The narrow wooden floor between the tatami and the garden acts as an *engawa*, the transitional space between the interior and the exterior. This was the view that the family wanted to replicate again when the parlor was reconstructed in its original location.

The Evolution of a Modern Home

When Japan opened to the world after the Meiji Revolution in 1868, it actively emulated architectural traditions from Germany and Great Britain. However, ideas of modernism did not take root in Japan till after the Second World War. Toshihiro Kamikozawa, the owner of this house, is a scholar of German literature well versed in the aesthetics of modernity and rationalism. His wife, a piano teacher, had lived in Germany during her childhood. Although built with Western materials and techniques, this one-storied, rectangular concrete box house has a calm sense of space reminiscent of traditional Japanese homes.

The Kamikozawa house was built in 1959, when Japan was just starting its successful climb from devastation during the war to its current prosperity. The Kamikozawas lived in a modest wooden house at that time, but wanted to own a home that reflected their ideals and optimism. When they saw the work of architect Kenji Hirose in a magazine, they knew that they had found the architect for their dream house. Hirose has been a pioneer in the modern Japanese construction industry and is well known for having designed the first series of buildings in Japan using light gauge steel structures. His original proposal was far above the budget set by Toshihiro Kamikozawa, who was only 32 years old at that time. However, both husband and wife worked with their architect—who was just a bit older—till they agreed on the plans, and completed a house that was quite radical for its time.

Since its construction, the Kamikozawa home has undergone several renovations because architectural technology and building materials in the 1950s were not sufficiently sophisticated for the ideas of the owners and their architect. Adding new insulation material, waterproofing and heating under the floors were some of the alterations that had to be made. Then in 1976, Tetsuo Jinbo, an architect in Hirose's office, helped carry out complete renovation of this house, including installation of new sash window frames and massive double-glass sliding doors. A new kitchen and some contemporary furniture pieces were added in 1992.

Utter simplicity is the core of the architectural design of the Kamikozawas' house as well as their lifestyle. Despite frequent renovations, the original concept of this house has endured. In a sense, each renovation has resulted in bringing the house closer to the minimalist ideal of the Kamikozawas. It would have cost them about three times less money and much less trouble to construct a new house, but the couple saw the evolution of this house as a reflection of the evolution of their own lives from the days when they were young and poor but full of hope. The house has very little storage space, but it is enough for the Kamikozawas, who make every effort not to accumulate things unnecessarily. They both keep only three sets of clothes for each season, and give away books soon after reading them. The interior reflects their aesthetic discipline and a lifestyle fashioned on the principle "Less is more." Articulated by the German architect Mies van der Rohe, this adage was the touchstone of modern architecture during the first three quarters of the 20th century.

Above: This corner serves as a kitchen and dining room. Installed in 1992, the built-in kitchen unit is from Poggenpohl, a well known German company. The dining table was custom designed for this space when the house was renovated in 1976. The prismatic lighting fixtures in the ceiling cast an artistic shadow on the wall and the slate floor.

Left: One part of this one-room house is used as a bedroom. This simple bed was custom designed for the room, and has been used since 1959. The concrete block partition wall on the right separates the toilet block from the rest of the house. The long steel and glass desk on the left was designed in 1976 to match the fixed glass windows that replaced the original masonry wall in front of desk shown on the previous page.

Above: A wide south-facing deck seen through the glass doors serves to extend the inner space when necessary. The doors slide on grooves located below the floor level on the deck side, so that the glass frames are hidden from view and the glass appears to float above the floor. Beyond the deck is the Kamikozawas' other classic German possession, a Mercedes SL500, parked in a garage built in 1979.

Left: Mrs Kamikozawa enjoys playing the game of Go. Developed about 4,000 years ago in China, the game is said to have been brought to Japan just before the seventh century. Heating was added under this slate floor during the renovation process.

A Cottage Shaped by Old Memories

Blessed with balmy weather and an abundance of hot springs, the Pacific coast of the Izu Peninsula is a popular resort area. Its central mountains have a lingering atmosphere of timeless solitude. Here, in an idyllic quiet forest stands a two-storey cottage with just 34 square meters of floor space. In spite of its small size, its serene ambience speaks to the spirit and provides an oasis away from the mundane world. The cottage is a retreat for art producer Sakura Mori and her family. It replaces a villa built by her parents in 1968. Her parents were both lawyers and very interested in art and architecture. When the villa needed reconstruction in 1998, her parents, who knew of their daughter's profound affection toward this house, entrusted the task of managing the design and construction of the cottage to her.

Given an opportunity of developing a concept for the new house, Mori decided to draw upon her childhood memories and experiences at the family summer villa, which were deeply etched in her mind. From her countless recollections, she singled out the one that had left the most indelible mark on her. This was the memory of the time when she was a little girl and had woken up in the dead of night to find herself surrounded by darkness. The pitch-black room had intimidated her. At that moment, she had her first consciousness of the existence of death. Mori believes that this incident has molded her view of life, as it was the fear of darkness, and the anxiety about what may come after, that made her aware of the importance of life. Mori asked Yasushi Horibe, an architect who is almost the same age as her, to design a new vacation home that incorporates her childhood memories. Although her experience was rather negative, she wanted the darkness in the cottage to signify not death but something meaningful such as renewal and rebirth.

One way to preserve the memories of the old house would have been to simply remodel it with the addition of new doors, windows and wall finishes. Another way was to reuse as much of the existing structure and material as possible in the making of a new structure. But Horibe chose neither alternative, deciding instead to create a completely new meditative space that would still be capable of invoking Mori's memories of the old house. The result is a contemporary new cottage with an undulating, dimly lit space that flows through the entire structure. There are no partitions, and the doors and windows have been sized and located so as to give the cottage a feeling of spaciousness. The cottage is pentagonal—which is unique in Japanese architecture—and sits on the same spot as Mori's old family villa. What is left of the old cottage is its environmental feel, its dreamy space, and the surrounding trees in an approximately 400-meter garden. For Mori, however, it has a spiritual significance and a personal reminiscence that makes it more than a rebirth of a private home. Mori and the architect created this house as if it were a piece of "art work," which means the house is not really for daily living, but for the art of remembering what has gone by, for giving time to oneself and for thinking about one's past as well as the future.

The pitched roof is visible inside, and aids in the dreamy flow of space, especially when the subdued light is reflected on the wall. Soft light comes into this room from the southeast window, which has been set deep into the room to shade it from direct sunlight.

Above: An FRP sculpture by Kyotaro Hakamata named "The Birth of Night" is displayed on the wall above the stairs.

Left: A dining room and a kitchen occupy the second floor. An axial pole is centered in the dining room as if to gather people around it. On sunny days, one can see the glittering sea from the window, far beyond the greenery. It is the same scene as was seen from the old house that was here before.

Opposite: The architect deliberately designed this window to be small, in order to frame and articulate a special part of the view outside.

A Room for Viewing Light and Shadows of Life

On a typical day in June, a gentle rain falls incessantly. Leaving the glass and *shoji* doors open, Doctor Shoei Sasao of Hadano City in Kanagawa Prefecture sits quietly in a very special room and looks out at the landscaped garden and the fresh, vivid verdure of rain-washed green leaves and lichen-covered tree trunks. Moist wind blows through the room, and faint sunlight and subdued light coming through opaque Japanese paper screens seem to mingle. The beauty of this traditional tatami room can be understood from such a glimpse into a day in the life of Doctor Shoei Sasao, who savors these contemplative hours to the full. He spends most of his free time in the room, where he reads books and meditates in deep repose. After enjoying a splendid day, he sleeps here at night.

Doctor Shoei Sasao partly reconstructed his house ten years ago in order to customize this room for his personal use. His old acquaintance, Shuri Kakinuma, who studied under the famous architect, Seiichi Shirai, designed this traditional room. Japanese architecture is in general very simple, therefore sensitivity to detail is all important. For example, the *shoji* doors made of thin wooden strips arranged in various rectangular patterns, are pasted with paper on the outside so that the beautiful latticework can be seen from inside the room. The sizes and proportions of frames, doors, brackets, and *hikite* (door handles) have all been designed to balance the space in the room.

Traditional techniques of decoration are also of utmost importance in a Japanese-style room. In this room, Kakinuma employed a special method for the ceiling which is covered with splints made of Japanese arborvitae, beautifully woven to form a striking pattern called *ajiro*. If the pattern had been made on a flat surface, the ceiling would have looked convex. So the central part of the ceiling was raised by 20 millimeters to compensate for the visual distortion. The floorboards of the *tokonoma* alcove are of lacquer layered in a manner referred to as *fuki-urushi*, in which the applied lacquer is wiped and dried before the next layer is applied, rendering the layers of lacquer translucent enough to allow the wood grain underneath to gradually show through.

Doctor Sasao's private garden is an integral part of this room, and an extension of the interior. While he often relaxes here in solitude, he occasionally invites his friends for conversation over some sake. In order to delight his guests as well as for his own pleasure, he arranges cut flowers from his garden in his favorite vase. This vase and the other items in the room were bought in antique shops or during his travels, and are aptly suited to his traditional room. Although he used to be very fond of going to Japanese inns, he has lost interest in them now, for nowhere does he feel more comfortable than in this very special room of his own.

Above: Glass and wood screen doors provide insulation from the outside world and can be adjusted to soften light and let the breeze in. When not used, these doors are designed to collapse into a niche in the wall. The deep eaves protect the interior from strong sunlight and rain when the screens are open.

Left: The calmness brought to the room by *shoji* doors and tatami mats is an important feature of this interior. A simple alcove with a raised floor, without the usual supporting *toko-bashira* helps achieve this sense of unobstructed space. Sasao gives utmost care to the art of nurturing *bonsai* trees, like this tiny pine tree in the *tokonoma*.

Top: The *fusuma* door (at left) has a special curved top, traditionally used for doors leading to tearooms.

Above: Hanging scrolls are changed frequently depending on the season and the mood of the room. When not in use, scrolls are carefully rolled and put away in wooden boxes specially designed for preserving them.

Right: What appears to be a simple tatami room is in fact quite special, and has a wealth of beautiful details. A part of the ceiling is covered with Japanese arborvitae splints, beautifully woven to form an intricate pattern. The hanging calligraphy scroll with the Chinese character, *ying*, for "firefly," is by the famous painter, Morikazu Kumagai. The wide *fusuma* doors hide a small kitchen behind them.

A Tribute to Masters of Modernism

Fusaichiro Inoue (1898–1993), who lived north of Tokyo in Takasaki City, was a well known patron of the arts and left behind a considerable legacy for the people of his hometown. After studying painting, sculpture and architecture in Paris, he returned to Takasaki City and founded a movement that promoted the use of Western design in traditional Japanese crafts for export.

Through his connection with the Modern Movement in Japan, Inoue came into contact with several important architects. In 1934 he invited the influential German architect Bruno Taut to Takasaki City. Taut helped popularize the use of Western motifs in Japanese arts and crafts, and later became a co-partner of the shop Inoue set up for selling textiles, tableware and home furnishings in Ginza. In 1945, as World War II ended, Inoue helped establish the Takasaki People's Orchestra, (now the Gunma Symphony Orchestra). The Gunma Music Center, where the Gunma Symphony Orchestra now performs, was also Inoue's brainchild. He proposed that Antonin Raymond (1888–1976) be the architect of the Music Center, which was completed in 1961. Incidentally, Inoue also influenced the choice of the architect for the Gunma Prefecture Museum of Modern Art, designed by Arata Isozaki in 1974.

Raymond was a Czech-born architect who migrated to the US to work with Frank Lloyd Wright, and accompanied Wright to Japan in 1919 to work on Tokyo's Imperial Hotel. Raymond stayed on in Japan after Wright left, designing over 400 buildings in the US and Japan. He became an important figure, one of the pioneers who introduced modern Western architecture to Japan. Inoue, who admired Raymond's creativity, befriended him before the war. When Inoue's house burned down in 1952, Inoue, with Raymond's permission, decided to build a replica of Raymond's newly completed house. Raymond's house was built in simple cubic forms representative of the early Modern Movement. Inoue's single-storey rectangular house stands behind a Japanese-style garden among bamboo trees and a stone lantern. It has a central patio with a living room on one side and the bedroom, a Japanese reception room and the kitchen on the other. A series of *shoji* doors gives the living room great versatility. When these doors are fully open to the terrace, one can enjoy a full view of the garden. Raymond designed the exposed cedar beams and halved diagonal timbers in this room. The walls are covered with rotary lauan veneers; while *shoji* doors and windows skirt the rooms. The low, overhanging eaves, 150 centimeters in depth, protect the *shoji* paper from rain and control the flow of light. The architect has used considerable skill in combining common construction materials and a simple interior, while harmonizing Japanese elements with Western modernism.

Inoue lived in this house for 41 years. After his death, the house was put up for public auction. With donations from local citizens grateful for Inoue's patronage of the arts, the foundation Inoue had set up while he was alive made a successful bid on the house, then restored the house to its original beauty. The Inoue House, now maintained by his foundation, has been open to the public since 2002.

Above: An unusually wide frameless *fusuma* separates the living room and hall. A Western-style stove in the room's center co-exists with Japanese wood and paper elements. North-facing *shoji* windows near the ceiling filter the sun's rays to create delicate plays of light and shadow in the room.

Right: A desk has been built-in at the north side of the living room. The halved diagonal cedar log beams recall a *minka* house. Raymond here skillfully combines Japanese and Western design features.

Previous pages: A series of *shoji* doors opens onto the patio, extending the interior outward. In a traditional Japanese house, *shoji* screens slide between posts, but can only open halfway. In contrast, the architect for this home designed a sill beyond the posts, so the *shoji* doors can open wider.

Above: In keeping with the philosophy of the owner and the architect, this simple building is in harmony with its environment. The stone-paved floor is protected by low, overhanging eaves. The eaves mimic the deep thatched overhangs common in traditional Japanese architecture to protect a house from frequent rain. There is no rainwater pipe, so a gravel channel has been designed in the garden to receive the rain as it drips from the roof.

Right: The patio facing the Japanese garden connects the two wings of the house, and is also used as an entrance hall.

A House with a View of Mount Asama

Karuizawa is a resort 150 kilometers northwest of Tokyo, in mountainous Nagano Prefecture. This sleepy little town, nestled 1,000 meters above sea level at the base of Mount Asama, became famous only after the British missionary Archdeacon AC Shaw happened to visit. Struck by its natural beauty reminiscent of his Scottish hometown, Shaw built a villa here in 1888. Since that time, Karuizawa, with its perfect summer weather, has been transformed into a popular retreat for Japan's elite. Just a stone's throw from the town center, rows of shops give way to majestic woods, while thick trees muffle the town's noises. Clouds rising from Mount Asama hang over Karuizawa Heights, giving it an almost mystical beauty.

The country house of Yoshikazu Suzuki is perched on a part of the Karuizawa mountainside that was recently developed for housing lots. Suzuki's lot has a beautiful view of Mount Asama, and, on its northern side, borders a deep valley's lush greenery. This narrow strip of land was not an easy site for a house because of its steep slope, but Suzuki fell in love with the beautiful view of Mount Asama from this location. He asked architect Yasushi Horibe to design a house for him here. After carefully considering the shape and inclination of the property and the view of Mount Asama from various points, Horibe developed the plan for the house. All existing big trees were to be left as they were found, with the house to be built nestled among them. The main room on the upper floor was designed around a big chestnut tree, almost like a theatre whose windows open onto the magnificent view of Mount Asama.

Modern architecture usually strives to achieve large column-free space. However, the architect chose to locate five rattan-covered wooden posts in the middle of the main saloon, reinforcing the feeling of it being a room in the forest. Horibe also believed that these posts would invite people to gather around them. The entrance porch leads directly to this saloon. Its wooden ceiling follows the slope of the roof that continues to the deep eaves. The result is an inviting ambiance, in which family and friends inadvertently find themselves relaxing against one of the columns while enjoying the view of Mount Asama.

One never tires of the opulent view of the outdoors from this house. The mountain scene changes from moment to moment and from day to day. Nature also unfolds its magic according to the rhythm of the seasons. A mantle of fresh green covers the hills in spring; the groves thicken their dark green leaves in summer; autumn clothes the forests in fiery colors; and a blanket of snow settles over the hillsides in winter. One wakes up to the sound of birds singing and an occasional entourage of them flying across the sky, veiled in the morning haze. The house silently stands on a hill surrounded by constantly varying cloud forms, as the day gives way to the evening glow. This retreat truly awakens the soul to the taste of true luxury.

Above: The architect has artfully combined
Western elements with traditional Japanese techniques to create this retreat. Wooden furniture
complements the natural wood ceiling, which is
also visible past the windows. The floor is covered
with the boards of *sawara* cypress, and the walls
are of white painted plaster.

Right: This modern space has the emotive quality
of traditional Japanese interiors. Five round columns
bound with rattan ropes accentuate the Japanese
mood. A Japanese-style low table surrounded by
four posts placed in the center of the sitting room
invites people to come together. Through wide
windows, one can see the deep valley, whose scene
changes from season to season. The physical division of space in a Japanese house occurs after a
roof is constructed. This is unlike Western buildings
where walls separating each room are built first.

Previous pages: This terrace has a panoramic view
of a deep valley. White birches, which grow abun-
dantly in Karuizawa Heights, stand next to the house.

Top right: The wooden ceiling shows rafters made of cedar on ribs of Japanese red pine.

Right: Here is a modern space with the soft light filtering through *shoji* screens, giving it a Japanese touch and a warm, welcoming feeling.

Left: These two poles together resemble the *torii*, a special gate seen at the entrance to Shinto shrines, invoking a sacred space amidst nature. Behind the columns stands a Western fireplace. Natural elements like fire were worshiped in ancient Japan.

Above: The tiled bathroom has a traditional wood tub. *Hiba* cedar is considered to be one of the best materials for a bath not just because of its resistance to water but also because of its fragrance. A place for relaxation, this bath has been designed to create the illusion of bathing in natural surroundings.

Left: The lower-level patio has a wide opening toward the terrace, and a horizontal slit on the southern wall made of American red cedar allows the breeze to flow through. This space cleverly exploits the topography of the land. The formwork for concrete was made of long wooden boards instead of plywood to achieve a richer texture. The harmony between the house's interior and exterior creates an ambience of peace and time-lessness as well as visual richness.

A New House and a Tree

Coming from a traditional potters' family in the culturally rich city of Kanazawa, Takuo Nakamura is one of the leading contemporary ceramic artists in Japan. One of his works—a freshwater jar (*mizusashi*) made in 2001—is showcased as part of the collection at the New York Metropolitan Museum of Art. Nakamura is prolific in his work and is constantly driven to invent new techniques and ideas. He revels in presenting a new range of works for almost every exhibition where his work is shown. For example, for one exhibition, he made a series of sculptures by partially mixing red and white clay, shaping it into a squarish form, and then slicing it up. Each surface of the sliced pieces was then rendered with spontaneous designs with a mottled effect. The white parts of these surfaces were then overglazed with vivid colors. For another series, he angled a long, thin sheet of clay to make U-shaped slabs, and left them on the ground to twist into random forms under their own weight. This "experiment" resulted in dynamic forms that charged the space around them.

Nakamura was raised in an old Western-style house which had one Japanese-style traditional drawing room built by his father, the renowned potter Nakamura Baizan (pages 214–223). To his surprise, Nakamura found that whatever he created seemed suitable for display in his father's *tokono-ma* in that particular room. Nakamura decided to discover his own artistic identity independent of Baizan's aesthetics by building his own home and atelier with no connection whatsoever to his father's house. Architect Hiroshi Naito helped give shape to this idea by creating a design that allows Nakamura's own personality to be vividly expressed.

Angular dynamism seen in Nakamura's sculptures is echoed in the design of Nakamura's new house. The first storey is built of reinforced concrete and the second and third stories have a steel-frame structure, in response to Kanazawa's snowy winters and soft ground. The first floor houses the guest room and the artist's studio, while the bedrooms are located on the second floor. The third floor is kept relatively open and is often used as an art gallery. Naito designed every room with attention to the harmonic interplay between surfaces, volumes and construction materials, making sure there was no overpowering dominant form in the house so that Nakamura may be able to imbue the house with his own creativity while at the same time draw inspiration from it.

The balance of natural and man-made beauty in his house was also important to the artist and his architect. Naito designed special windows to frame the views of the 400-year-old pine tree located in the garden between the new house and the old cottage belonging to Nakamura's father. Naito also left the finishing and furnishings of the house to the owner. According to Nakamura, it took him two years to select a dining table suitable for the room. After moving into his new house in 1996, Nakamura has been developing his ideas of creating and defining spaces by using his sculptures. This house will no doubt continue to be a partner in Nakamura's creativity in the years to come.

Paper is usually put only on the outside of *shoji* doors. However, in Nakamura's house both sides of the *shoji* have been papered over to subdue the sunlight more effectively. Nakamura's sculptures and flower arrangements have been displayed here as if in a *tokonoma* alcove, showing his ability to create Japanese-style spaces within his modern home. *Shoji* doors also serve as a kind of wall illumination for Nakamura's works.

Above: The bedroom on the second floor has a marble floor. Nakamura decided to take the time needed to furnish his house exactly the way he likes it. The bed was designed by the owner himself.

Right: The square window was designed to frame the view of the green leaves and the large trunk of the 400-year-old Japanese pine tree. Nakamura's father's cottage also looks onto this tree from the other side.

Previous pages: The third floor is dramatic in its severity, and is often used as an art gallery. The floor is made of medium-density fiber boards (MDF), on which lacquer (*urushi*) has been applied. Matsuo Daitani created the modern light fixture for this room.

Above: Nakamura drew inspiration from rafters dumped on construction sites, and created this sculpture series named "Taruki" (rafters). The deep brown earth tone of these artifacts was overglazed with five traditional colors (red, yellow, green, blue and purple) called *gosai* in Japanese.

Left: The white walls are well contrasted by the dark floor made of solid broadleaf boards. Ink-dyed *shoji* doors are unique in their design, but perfectly suited to this modern building, allowing air to circulate while screening out the light. The table seen through the door was designed by Carlo Scarpa. Nakamura modified it by replacing the original glass tabletop with a black board. *Shoji* doors lead to a red gravel court and Nakamura's workroom.

Right: This clay-colored piece of pottery, painted with resplendent enamel designs, was originally created as a plate. Here, it holds graceful flowers and wiry leaves.

Many thanks to Anna Sherman and Nina Sheth Nanavaty who helped with the editing; Kazue Shibuya for helping with the photoshoots; Kinya Sawada, Hitoshi Imai, Yoshifumi Takeda for showing us some splendid houses; Koshi Baba for introducing Murata and Tada to each other; Masakazu Fujii for the advice on graphic design; Mikiko Morozumi for helping with the translation; Kasumi Yamamoto Stewart for his words of wisdom; Ikuyo Toyonaga, Akiko Yamazaki and Yoichi Tada, who has been a great encouragement. Last but not least, we'd like to say thank you to all the architects, the homeowners and their families for their assistance and co-operation.

Noboru Murata
Kimie Tada
Geeta Mehta

Bibliography

Addis, Stephen, *How to Look at Japanese Art*. New York: Harry N Abrams Inc., 1996.

Akira Naito and Takeshi Nishikawa, *Katsura—A Princely Retreat*. Tokyo, London and New York: Kodansha International, 1984.

Black, Alexandra and Noboru Murata, *The Japanese House: Architecture and Interiors*. Boston, Vermont and Tokyo: Tuttle Publishing, 2000.

Bring, Mitchell and Wayembergh, Josse, *Japanese Gardens: Design and Meaning*. New York: McGraw-Hill, 1981.

Elisseeff, Danielle and Elisseeff, Vadime, *Art of Japan*, New York: Harry N Abrams, Inc., 1985.

Friedman, Mildred and Abrams, Harry, *Tokyo Form and Spirit*. New York: Walker Art Publishers Center, Harry N Abrams Inc., 1986.

The Heibonsha Survey of Japanese Art (all volumes). Chicago: Art Media Resources.

Heino, Engel, *Measure and Construction of the Japanese House*. Boston, Vermont and Tokyo: Tuttle Publishing, 1989.

Ienaga Saburo, *Japanese Art: A Cultural Appreciation*. Tokyo: John Weatherhill Inc., 1979.

Iwatate, Marcia and Conran, Terence, *Eat.Work. Shop.: New Japanese Design*. Singapore, Hong Kong and Indonesia: Periplus Editions, 2004.

Kakudo, Yoshiko, *The Art of Japan*. San Francisco: Chronicle Books, 1991.

Katoh, Amy Sylvester and Shin Kimura, *Japan Country Living: Spirit, Tradition, Style*. Boston, Vermont and Tokyo: Tuttle Publishing, 2002.

Kidder, Edward Jr, *The Art of Japan*. London: Century Publications, 1985.

Mahoney, Jean; Peggy Landers, Rao, *At Home with Japanese Design: Accents, Structure, and Spirit*. Boston, Vermont and Tokyo: Tuttle Publishing, 2001.

Mason, Penelope, *History of Japanese Art*. New Jersey: Prentice Hall/Harry N Abrams Inc., 1993.

Morse, Edward S, *Japanese Homes and Their Surroundings*. Boston, Vermont and Tokyo: Tuttle Publishing, 1989.

Nishi Kazuo and Hozumi Kazuo, *What is Japanese Architecture?* Translated by H Mack Horton. Tokyo, London and New York: Kodansha International, 1996.

Paine, Robert Treat and Soper, Alexander, *The Art and Architecture of Japan*. New Haven: Yale University Press, 1981.

Smith, Bradley, *A History of Japanese Art*. Tokyo: John Weatherhill Inc., 1971.

Stanley-Baker, Joan, *Japanese Art*. New York: Thames and Hudson, 2000.

Stewart, David, *The Making of Modern Japanese Architecture—1868 to the Present*. Tokyo, London and New York: Kodansha International, 1987.